HOW TO
HAVE A
WHOLE

IN A
BROKEN
WORLD

Other books by the author:

How to Say No to a Stubborn Habit
Managing Your Emotions
When a Good Man Falls
Living with Your Passions

HOW TO HAVE A WHOLE HEART IN A BROKEN WORLD

ERWIN LUTZER

While this book is designed for the reader's personal enjoyment and profit, it also is intended for group study. A Leader's Guide with Victor Multiuse Transparency Masters is available from your local bookstore or from the publisher.

VICTOR BOOKS ®

A DIVISION OF SCRIPTURE PRESS PUBLICATIONS INC.
USA CANADA ENGLAND

Most Scripture quotations in this book are from the *New American Standard Bible*, © the Lockman Foundation 1960, 1962, 1963, 1968, 1971, 1972, 1973, 1975, 1977. A few are from the *King James Version* (KJV).

Recommended Dewey Decimal Classification: 226.5; 248
Suggested Subject Headings: CHRISTIAN WALK; UPPER ROOM
DISCOURSE
Library of Congress Catalog Card Number: 87-81025
ISBN: 0-89693-025

Contents

This one is for Lori, Lynn, and Lisa,
who double all my joys, halve my sorrows,
and triple my expenses.

Preface:
Picking
Up
The
Pieces

Y ou've heard the saying, "I complained that I had no shoes until I met someone who had no feet."

That's how I feel when I meet people with broken hearts and emotional scars. In recent days:

- I counseled a young man who is searching for his father whom he has not seen in twenty-seven years. When this man's parents divorced when he was twelve months old, the agreement was that the father would never come back to his family. Now the son is obsessed with finding his dad, dead or alive.

- I communicated with a woman whose husband left her for another woman, handing her a divorce as a "Christmas present."

- I wrote to encourage a girl who was sexually molested by her father and then thrown out of the home.

The list could go on. With the breakup of the family

and the rise in child abuse, we can't begin to calculate the emotional damage that this generation faces. All we know is that these hurts run deeper and last longer than previously imagined.

What does Christ have to say to this generation? In the Upper Room, He comforted His disciples by saying, "Let not your hearts be troubled." And then He went on to give reasons why troubled hearts could remain calm: confused minds could be made stable, and bruised emotions could be healed.

To have a whole heart in a broken world does not imply perfection. Nor does it mean we live in perpetual emotional tranquility, for Christ Himself was often troubled in spirit.

A whole heart means that we can use our hurts as stepping-stones rather than stumbling blocks. The past can become a rudder, not an anchor; a cradle of new life rather than a coffin of death.

A whole heart means that we can experience inner resources for outward pressures. Like the woman at the well whose many marriages had collapsed, we can find "a well of water springing up into eternal life." The fruit of the Spirit is a description of emotional and spiritual wholeness.

Emotional and spiritual stability does not come easily to those who have been deeply hurt. But Christ's message is one of hope and power. Healing may come slowly, but *it will come.*

Here's the testimony of a single girl who was sexually abused by her father, unfavorably compared to her sister, and rejected by her mother:

On Monday, I cried and literally shook as I begged Jesus to help me. I felt as if God had stripped me of the shell I had so tightly encased around my inner self and what was left was a trembling, frightened little girl exposed to the Great God of heaven and earth. Once He stripped away everything I clung to and I was completely empty, He came last night to indwell me in a way that I can't even explain. He wanted to love the real me, not the counterfeit I tried to offer Him and everyone else. "Old things have passed away, behold all things have become new." Jesus does love even the worst of us. I am not afraid anymore for people to see my vulnerabilities. The old is gone forever. I can delight in insult, in hardships, in persecutions, in difficulties, for when I am weak, then am I strong.

In the Upper Room Christ spoke intimately with His friends. He left a message all of us need to hear—a message of forgiveness, fruitfulness, prayer, persecution, and hope. Our broken world needs to ponder His words.

Thousands can testify that He can make any one of us whole if we give Him all the pieces.

As children bring their broken toys,
With tears for us to mend,
I brought my broken dreams to God,
Because He was my friend.

But then, instead of leaving Him
In peace to work alone,
I hung around and tried to help
With ways that were my own.

At last, I snatched them back and cried,
"How can you be so slow?"
"My child," He said, "What could I do?
You never did let go."

—Author unknown

CHAPTER 1

GETTING AND KEEPING A CLEAN HEART

JOHN 13:1-32

Broken hearts are everywhere. Here is a letter I received from a young woman who heard a message I gave on the radio:

Greetings. This past Sunday I turned on the radio and heard you describe a situation that resembled mine. I am an ex-prostitute and a recovering alcoholic.

When I left prostitution, I was not able (because of children) to keep a job, so I didn't work for a over a year. I lost everything I had—apartment, car, furniture, and bank account. I lived on the street with my four-year-old daughter, though I didn't return to prostitution.

I took the last money I had, rented a motel room for two days, and came out a whole new person. I knew that Jesus had set me free from alcoholism. Within months, I had a job and became a trusted member of my family (they knew only about the alcoholism, not the prostitution).

For a year, I knew that God was keeping me safe, allowing me to heal completely. Unfortunately, I began to think that I could commit some small sins because I had been saved out of some big ones. So I began to lie and have occasional sexual encounters. I began not liking myself again. Exactly a year to the day of my meeting with God in the motel room, I began to drink again.

I thought I had lost God. For two months I mourned for God like one mourns the death of a loved one. I thought of suicide because I had no reason to live, except for my daughter who was then five years old.

One night in desperation I begged God to take me back. Then and there, I learned something: good works do not save a person. We are saved by grace through faith. I cannot do enough good things to be forgiven. I cannot cover my sins with good works.

I faced two problems: First, I didn't think I was worthy of salvation, and so I shouldn't take the gift. Then, second, after I accepted Christ, I thought He had left me after I sinned.

Now I know that God didn't leave me. I also know that God has forgiven me, and that He will always take me back. Regardless of my past, Christ has made me clean.

"Regardless of my past, Christ has made me clean!" Of course, God can forgive and restore prostitutes and drug users. If He cannot, then the Gospel is not good news.

Ironically, Jesus taught that it is easier for such people to be forgiven than for those who think they have committed only small sins. The ones who think they need no forgiveness are the ones whose need is the greatest.

To have a whole heart in a broken world, we must be

reconciled to God by accepting the gift of salvation through Christ. But the next step is *to know how to keep spiritually clean by accepting Christ's cleansing every single day.*

A basic axiom is that *we tend to repeat sins we feel guilty about.* That's why the cleansing of the past is so necessary for victory in the future.

■ The Effects of Sin

On the morning of January 15, 1986, an arsonist broke into Moody Church in Chicago. He stole some things from my office, then decided to set the organ, piano, pulpit, and seven oak chairs on fire.

By the time firemen arrived, nothing was left of the two instruments. The organ was reduced to a few bits of metal in an ash heap, the piano to a metal frame. There wasn't a trace of the pulpit or chairs—except, of course, the ashes.

Smoke damage throughout the church was extensive. Cleaning the building took thousands of man-hours. No matter how often we cleaned the seats in the auditorium, or the books and desks in our offices, we would still find soot hiding in the crevice of a chair or desk drawer.

Incredibly, the actions of one man (which probably took ten minutes) caused grime to settle on 4,000 auditorium seats and hymnals, the walls and ceiling, not to mention the many Sunday School rooms and offices of the church. Though the arsonist was arrested and spent time in jail, the consequences of his crime were thereby not diminished.

Just so, in the Garden of Eden, Adam, by one act of disobedience, caused the smudge of sin to fall on every human heart. And throughout the centuries, man has tried to get himself clean.

Try as we might, we cannot erase the stains. The smudge of sin has settled in the human spirit, a place that cannot be reached by popular detergents. The resolve to do better next time; the attempt to forget the sins of the past; even therapy that is supposed to help us face our past—none of this can take away the sins of rejection and the guilt that settle like fog over the human psyche.

Alcohol may temporarily deaden the conscience; sensuality may for a moment divert the attention; resolution to do better may give a glimmer of hope; but the *stain* is still there.

For peace of mind, we have to know that our past has been put away forever. We need the assurance that our relationship with God has been permanently settled. We also need a clear conscience so that we can be at peace with ourselves.

The first step in living clean is to *be* clean. Since we focus our minds on whatever makes us feel guilty, we will repeat our sins unless we know that the smudge is gone. Guilt leads to failure, failure to more guilt. Someone has aptly called it "the cycle of the damned."

"I died by the inch inside," said the young woman who was living in immorality. Her conscience and training told her it was wrong, but she felt trapped. One part of her wanted to be clean; the other could not face breaking the relationship. Her unsuccessful struggle is best described as the shriveling of the soul.

But there is hope!

Christ came to give us a cleansing that goes to the depths of the human conscience. To *be* forgiven and to *feel* forgiven is the privilege of every one of us. When Christ washed the disciples' feet, He taught what cleansing means.

■ The Illustration

If we were accustomed to walking dusty roads with open sandals, we could better appreciate the ancient custom of washing the feet of guests when they showed up at the door. One day, when Christ and His disciples got to the Upper Room, there was no servant waiting. So they sat down, each probably expecting the other to perform this courtesy. The supper ended, but still no one would play the servant's role.

No one, that is, except the Master Himself.

After supper, Christ took off His outer garments, girded Himself with a towel, and began washing the disciples' feet. Why did He have the grace to play the role of a servant? Servanthood was actually the sum total of His mission. We read, "Jesus, knowing that the Father had given all things into His hands, and that He had come forth from God, and was going back to God" (John 13:3). Notice His unswerving confidence—He had come from the Father for a specific purpose and would soon be returning to the Father in triumph. That assurance enabled Him to bow unpretentiously before His disciples and wash their dirty feet. The Creator was washing the feet of the creature!

Possibly, Peter was the last one in the semicircle. So he asked, "Lord, do You wash my feet?" (v. 6)

"What I do, you do not realize now, but you shall understand hereafter" (v. 7).

Peter was embarrassed. Something was wrong! Servants wash the feet of kings; kings do not wash the feet of servants.

"Never shall You wash my feet!" (v. 8a)

Christ did not honor Peter's wish. More was at stake here than meets the untrained eye. What Peter saw happening before him had a deeper meaning than the mere washing of feet.

"If I do not wash you, you have no part with Me" (v. 8b).

What could *that* possibly mean? To refuse Christ's courtesy is to forfeit friendship, or even worse, be permanently separated from Him!

"Lord, not my feet only but also my hands and my head!" (v. 9)

But Peter misunderstood the symbolism. He had already had a bath; he didn't need another one. Only his feet were dirty. So Christ explained, "He who is bathed needs only to wash his feet, but is completely clean; and you are clean, but not all of you" (v. 10).

With that, Christ washed Peter's feet and sat down to give a further explanation of what He had just done. This is an illustration of spiritual cleansing, and an example of humility and service.

Clean feet are a picture of a clean heart. The dust of the streets is symbolic of the smudge of the world. Christ is teaching what it means to be cleansed, and also the need to distinguish between a bath and having one's feet washed.

Let's ask Christ some specific questions about getting and staying clean.

■ Who Needs to Be Cleansed?

Every Christian needs to be cleansed. Peter needed it and so do we.

But why did Christ tell Peter that he didn't need a whole bath? Obviously, if a little washing is good, more washing would seemingly be better.

There are two spiritual washings. The first is the bath of regeneration. That happens when we receive Christ as Saviour. It's an act of God whereby we are made members of God's family. At that moment we are born again, and God declares us to be as righteous as Christ Himself is! This bath cleanses us forever; we need it only once. In fact, this washing takes away our sins past, present, and future, since He has "canceled out the certificate of debt consisting of decrees against us and which was hostile to us; and He has taken it out of the way, having nailed it to the cross" (Col. 2:14).

But there is a second kind of washing. It's the subjective cleansing that happens when we are willing to admit our specific sins in the sight of God. The first washing means that we are legally clean; the second means that our conscience is free from guilt. The first happens only once; the second is repeated as often as we need it, even several times a day.

Christians who think that the first washing has to be repeated teach that we actually lose our standing before God every time we sin. Dr. Harry Ironside, a former pastor of Moody Church, told of a man who claimed that he had been saved 99 times! With such theology, the man would probably have to be saved another 999 times! What is more, I hope he is saved on the *day* he dies. If he gets saved on Sunday, but dies on Monday, he might be in trouble, according to his theology.

In the Greek text, Christ uses two separate words for washing. "He who has bathed (*louō*) needs only to wash (*niptō*) his feet, but is completely clean; and you are clean, but not all of you" (v. 10). Yes, there is a difference between a bath and getting your feet washed. Those who have been bathed do not have this act repeated. Judas, He said, had never had a bath; the rest of the disciples had.

To have your feet washed is another story. We may need that 99 times, or 999 times. We've all become conscious of sins committed after coming to Christ. And although those sins do not deprive us of our legal acceptance before God, they do put us out of moral agreement with God. In other words, we are out of fellowship.

The impurity of the world! We rub against it everywhere. And just when we think it is gone, it shows up in unexpected places. Sensuality, lust, pride, covetousness: these are the desires that arise in our hearts.

■ How Are We Cleansed?

How do we get Christ to reach down and clean away the smudge that settles down so deeply in the human heart? *Agreement* is the key word. "If we confess our sins, He is faithful and just to forgive our sins and to cleanse us from all unrighteousness" (1 John 1:9).

That word *confess* means "to agree together." We must say the same thing about our condition as God does; we must be in complete moral agreement with Him. Taking such a perspective on our sins means that we admit our guilt without any self-justification. We also admit that only Christ can cleanse us.

Recently, I spoke with a woman who had had an abortion. Though she had confessed her sin to God, she still felt polluted. She was forgiven, but she was not cleansed.

So how can we be cleansed? Here are some basics we must never forget.

First, Christ's sacrifice on the cross was complete. There is no sin too big for God to forgive. The woman previously mentioned thought that abortion was the "unpardonable sin." But no sin, strictly speaking, is unpardonable—unless it is the sin of unbelief. When we see our sins as greater than Christ's death, we forfeit forgiveness. But it is *we* who think our sins are so great that the cross could not possibly have included them! We may even believe that it is a mark of humility to think that our sins are greater than God's grace. But if we doubt God's ability to forgive, that's pride and unbelief, not humility.

Here are a few lines from a letter I received from a

troubled young man: "On Saturday night, I was tempted to commit the unpardonable sin. I became angry and started cursing God and calling the Holy Spirit a blasphemous, insulting name. I asked for forgiveness and things didn't seem right, so I became more angry. I was getting God very angry and insulting the Holy Spirit. Do you think I might have committed the unpardonable sin?"

I'm glad I was able to tell this young man that he had not committed a sin that was unpardonable. In fact, what apparently brought on the anger was the sin of pornography he mentioned later in the letter. The fact that he had a desire to come back to God was, in itself, a fairly reliable indication that this young man had not committed the unpardonable sin. If he wanted forgiveness, he could have had it.

Whenever we think we have sinned too greatly to be forgiven, we are doubting the foresight of God. We are assuming that He did not consider the particularly scandalous sins His people would commit. The Bible teaches that some sins are greater than others: "Jesus answered, 'You would have no authority over Me, unless it had been given from above; for this reason he who delivered Me up to you has the greater sin'" (John 19:11). But it is not more difficult for God to forgive a bigger sin than a smaller one. The blood of Christ has no restrictions so far as forgiveness is concerned.

A sin too great to forgive is a contradiction in the presence of God's grace. "Where sin abounds, grace abounds all the more" (cf. Rom. 5:20).

Second, we must agree that God is *faithful* to forgive. The woman who had an abortion confessed her sin many times, but still was unsure whether she had been cleansed. Whether she realized it or not, she was doubting the trustworthiness of God's promises. Like Satan in the Garden of Eden, she was questioning whether or not God's Word is dependable.

There is a better way. If you have confessed your sin, but still feel guilty, memorize verses of Scripture which assure that God forgives those who depend humbly on His mercy. "How blessed is he whose transgression is forgiven, whose sin is covered! How blessed is the man to whom the Lord does not impute iniquity, and in whose spirit there is no deceit!" (Ps. 32:1-2)

If guilty feelings continue, realize that Satan is acting out his role of accuser of the brethren. One day when I was feeling agitated and guilty, I asked God to search my heart, but no unconfessed sin surfaced in my consciousness. Finally, I realized my guilt was coming from Satan, not the Holy Spirit. The difference is that the Holy Spirit always points out specific unconfessed sin; Satan always brings to mind sins already confessed or gives us a vague, undefined sense of guilt. So I said out loud, "Be gone, Satan, for it is written, 'Who will bring a charge against God's elect? God is the One who justifies; who is the One who condemns? Christ Jesus is He who died, yes, rather who was raised, who is at the right hand of God, who also intercedes for us' " (Rom. 8:33-34). In a moment, the guilt left.

Don't let Satan rob you of your cleansing.

■ What Is the Purpose of Cleansing?

Jesus said to Peter, "If I do not wash you, you have no part with Me" (v. 8). As a believer, Peter was already joined to his Master, and after the Ascension would be a member of Christ's body, of His flesh and of His bones. When Christ said that washing was necessary to have a part with Him, He was referring to *fellowship*. This is the way the word *part* is used in Luke 10:42 where Christ commends Mary for having chosen "the good part," namely fellowship with Himself.

Peter loved Christ. Responding to his Master's invitation to come to Him, Peter was able to participate in the miracle of walking on water (Matt. 14:29); later he spoke with courage, "Thou art . . . the Son of the Living God" (Matt. 16:16). But soon he would fail Christ, denying that he even knew Him!

Peter's greatest grief would be that he was out of fellowship with his Saviour. He would have to be cleansed. There would have to be restoration; the friendship would need to be repaired.

But that's the purpose of washing—it's that we might be able to walk with Christ without barriers between us. "Behold, I stand at the door and knock; if any one hears My voice and opens the door, I will come in to him, and will dine with him, and he with Me" (Rev. 3:20). That's Christ's invitation to a church that had long since fallen in love with the world. The Saviour invites individuals within the fellowship to leave the world to eat with Him, spiritually speaking. But you can't come to His table with a dirty heart.

Have you ever had lunch with someone who disagreed with you, or even disliked you? You are glad when it's over. But to share a meal with a friend is a treat; time stands still; you are in fellowship; you might even be in love. And that's exactly the relationship that Christ wants with His followers.

■ How Often Should We Be Cleansed?

You can scarcely put your foot down in this world without kicking up dust. The thoughts of the mind, the words of our mouths—all of these interfere with the Holy Spirit who desires that we be in fellowship with the Saviour. Yet, regrettably, many Christians live out of fellowship with Christ. Here are some reasons why:

1. *"I'm going to mess up anyway."*

Some Christians allow their sins to pile up. Perhaps they began the day by confessing sins, but by midmorning, they bend under the pressures of work or physical human needs. So they think, "There's no use confessing sins. I don't stay in fellowship long enough to make it worthwhile."

Immaturity. That characterizes those who don't realize that we must learn to live in fellowship with Christ regardless of how many times we fail. Christ died for failures. When you learned to walk, you fell many times. One young man, struggling with perverted sexual temptations, told me that he practiced confessing to God sinful thoughts whenever they tried to occupy his mind. And eventually, he sensed that God had given him victory. The power of sin was broken because he learned not merely to keep "short accounts" with God, but rather "current accounts" with God. Confession must become a way of life.

2. *"I've committed the same sin so many times that I feel embarrassed to come to God about the same matter."*

Unbelief. That distinguishes those who don't know that God has promised to forget sins that He has forgiven. It is we who speak about confessing the same sin again and again. God says, "What sin?" He doesn't remember yesterday.

3. *"I'll get back in fellowship when I'm sure I will be able to hold out."*

Ignorance. Who among us is ever sure that we will "hold out"? When we confess our sin, God requires that we sincerely want to be rid of that sin, and agreeing with Him means we give Him permission to remove it from our lives forever. But we don't have to promise that we will never do it again, though that should be our intention when we confess a besetting sin. Yet, it's really not us who hold on to Christ; He holds onto us when we focus on Him.

4. *"I want to enjoy the world first before I settled down to serious commitment to Christ."*

Deception. It's a strong word but it fits. Whenever we believe that the pleasures of sin outweigh those on God's right hand, we are believing a lie and open our lives up to the discipline of God. Both in this world and especially in the world to come, we will discover that sin is never a bargain. Luther said it well when he pointed out it is not possible to willfully commit a sin without first thinking wrongly about God.

■ How Hard Is It to Be Cleansed?

In one sense, cleansing is easy; in another, it is very difficult. Peter did not want Christ to wash his feet. Would you honestly want someone to wash your dirty feet? Probably not.

Some Christians think Christ was giving an ordinance to the church because He told the disciples that they should do to one another as He had done to them (vv. 14-15). I respect those who believe this, but doesn't His teaching refer to the inner humble attitude of service we should have for others? The only other place foot-washing is referred to in the New Testament is in 1 Timothy 5:10, where it does not refer to a ceremony but to charitable deeds for the poor.

Those who do believe it is a valid ordinance have a foot-washing ceremony in church a few times a year—women in one room, men in another. Before the service, most of them do as you or I would: they wash their own feet! It's one thing to have your clean feet washed by someone else; it's quite another to have someone wash your dirty feet!

We all resist humility. And coming to Christ to have our hearts washed is not an easy matter. It's a blow to our own pride in this day when the masses have gone wild with self-help seminars and techniques that explore human potential. The New Age movement teaches that man's problem is not sin, but ignorance. To admit to sin is humiliating.

And how should we "wash one another's feet" as Christ commanded? One way is to serve one another in humility, as Christ did. "Do nothing from selfishness or empty conceit, but with humility of mind let each of you regard one another as more important than himself; do not merely look out for your own personal interests, but also for the interests of others" (Phil. 2:3-4).

Day by day, God gives us many opportunities to wash one another's feet. Through the example of lowly service, we are motivated to care for one another as Christ cared for His disciples.

■ What about Judas?

But there was one man who was not cleansed. Christ said to Peter, "You are clean, but not all of you" (v. 10b). John, who is recording this story for us, adds, "For He knew the one betraying Him; for this reason He said, 'Not all of you are clean'" (v. 11).

Peter needed his feet washed; Judas never had a bath. One of the Twelve was an apostate. That's not a conclusion that we can make just by looking at the outside. Judas, apparently, was able to do the same miracles as the other disciples, and was such a crafty hypocrite that he did not attract special notice. When Christ said to the group, "One of you shall betray Me," to their everlasting credit they did not suspect Judas, but asked, "Is it I?" (Matt. 26:21-22, KJV)

Peter gestured to John, who was sitting next to Christ; John in turn asked Christ who the culprit was. Christ said, "That is the one for whom I shall dip the morsel, and give it to him" (v. 26). So Judas was identified. Satan had already entered into his heart, and Judas then left to do the dastardly deed. You know the rest of the story. He betrayed Christ to the chief priests for thirty pieces of silver. Then after he saw that Christ was condemned, he did what 25,000 Americans do each year: he committed suicide.

What is the final epitaph of Judas? It is the same as that which could be written on the gravestone of every single human being who has never been bathed by Christ: *"It Would Have Been Good For That Man If He Had Not Been Born"* (Matt. 26:24).

Judas needed a bath, but did not let Christ give him one. Peter was bathed but needed his feet washed.

If you are not a born-again Christian, do not begin by confessing your sins to God—that's getting your feet washed. You must be bathed first; getting your feet washed comes later. Tens of thousands of people who confess their sins regularly are lost forever. God does not save those who begin by confessing individual sins. For one thing, you couldn't possibly remember them all; for another, you would have to begin again tomorrow. No matter how many times you have your feet washed, it is still not a bath.

The bath of regeneration makes you a new person. You receive the righteousness of Christ which makes you acceptable to God forever.

If you have never had a spiritual bath, transfer your trust to Christ right now. At this moment, admit that you are guilty of sin and want God's cleansing and forgiveness; place all of your faith in Him, and He will save you and make you one of His own. After that, you can begin the long process of spiritual growth, a process that will include many cleansing foot-washings along the path of life.

If you are already a believer, come to Christ to have your feet washed. The first step in having a whole heart is to be made clean daily through genuine confession.

What He did for Peter physically, He now does for us spiritually.

Let Him.

CHAPTER 2

ESTABLISHING A CALM HEART

JOHN 13:33–14:7

Don't you wish you could turn anxiety on and off like a faucet? Wouldn't it be great if you could worry from 9:30 P.M. to 10 P.M. and then shut it down so that you could get a good night's rest?

Unfortunately, we cannot control anxiety; anxiety arises from within and is not subject to reason or the dictates of the human will. Rather than playing the role of a humble servant, it comes to take charge over the whole person. Like most dictators, it refuses compromise. We need a power greater than ourselves to bid it adieu.

When Christ told His disciples that He would be leaving them, they were filled with anxiety and fear. "Little children, I am with you a little while longer. You shall seek Me; and as I said to the Jews, 'Where I am going, you cannot come,' now I say to you also" (John 13:33).

Peter asked for more details. "Lord, where are You going?" Christ replied, "Where I go, you cannot follow Me now; but you shall follow Me later" (v. 36). Peter's response was to promise Christ that he was willing to die, saying, "I will lay down my life for you" (v. 37). Christ was unimpressed; He predicted that Peter would deny Him instead.

Fear gripped the hearts of the disciples when they realized that Jesus was leaving them. The thought of coping with hostile religious leaders on their own was more than they could bear. What is more, Christ had woven His way into their hearts. They loved Him.

Ela Wheeler Wilcox once heard the comment that the same wind that blows a vessel west can also blow one east, depending on how the sail is set. Out of that bit of information came these lines:

One ship drives east and another drives west
With the selfsame winds that blow
'Tis the set of the sails
And not the gales
Which tells us the way to go.

Like the winds of the sea are the ways of fate
As we voyage along through life
'Tis the set of the soul
That decides its goal
And not the calm or strife.

The disciples had been given an object lesson on how they could keep their hearts *clean;* now they needed some instruction on how to keep their hearts *calm.* They would have to set their sail correctly to ride out the storm.

"Let not your heart be troubled," Christ began. Troubled hearts—the world is full of them. A woman suspects she has cancer, but can't bring herself to go to the doctor for fear that he will confirm those suspicions. A man is frightened believing he might lose his job; and another is wrenched knowing that his child is running away from God; and still another that his marriage is about to break up.

Many people are terrorized by anxiety, but cannot identify the object of their fears. In fact, anxiety has been called the official emotion of our age and the basis of much neurosis. Like a blip on a television screen, anxious thoughts can flit across our minds without permission.

The disciples were about to sink beneath the waves. That's why Christ turned their attention toward the certainty of their final destination. When everything is going well, heaven seems distant and even irrelevant. But when the big winds blow—when the doctor tells you that you've got only three months, or when you are overcome by loneliness—heaven becomes ever so welcome. It's then that we are keenly aware that the separations we experience here on earth will come to an end. A young woman who lost her father in a plane accident said, "What keeps me going is the knowledge that I will see my dad again." Most of us think the worst that could happen to us is an untimely death. If we can overcome that fear, the lesser ones will take care of themselves. But sometimes between our life today and eventual death all kinds of other storms cross our path. So Christ, knowing what's going on in the hearts of the disciples, pours a healing balm on troubled hearts.

"Let not your heart be troubled; believe in God, believe also in Me" (John 14:1). Christ linked Himself directly with God: He asked His disciples to trust in Him just as they trusted in God. He discussed His own departure to heaven and assured the disciples that someday they would join Him there. Christ knew that His followers become controlled by what they gaze at. So He turned the attention of the disciples to the glories of the future.

■ A Special Place

"In My Father's house are many dwelling places; if it were not so, I would have told you; for I go to prepare a place for you" (14:2). Heaven is a special place. The King James translation *many mansions* elicits the vision of a ranch style home with a fifty-acre front yard and limousines parked in the driveway. But the word *mansion* really means "dwelling place" and is used only one other time in all the New Testament—in verse 23 of John 14: "If anyone loves Me, he will keep My Word and My Father will love him, and we will come to him, and make Our abode with him." That word *abode* is the same word translated "mansion" or "dwelling place." Christ's point is that heaven has sufficient room for us all. Yes, it will be beautiful, but the disciples were not concerned about that—it was being reunited with Christ that was uppermost in their minds.

Nor should we think that Christ has been working for 2,000 years getting heaven ready for us. It has been facetiously suggested that since Christ was a carpenter on earth, He's been exercising the same skill in glory—He is working to finish the rooms in time for our arrival!

As God, He didn't have to get a head start. He can create our future home in a moment of time. Christ's point is simply, "I am leaving, and while I am gone, I will be preparing a place for you" (v. 3). Just as a mother prepares for the arrival of her son who has been at sea, so Christ is preparing for our arrival. Even now, it is ready for us.

Christ stresses that it will have plenty of room. The size of the New Jerusalem given in the Book of Revelation is 1,500 miles square and 1,500 miles high (21:16). If we take this literally, heaven will comprise thousands of stories, each one having an area almost as big as the United States. Divide that up into separate condominiums, and you have plenty of room for all the people who have ever lived since the beginning of time. The Old Testament saints—Abraham, Isaac and Jacob—they shall be there. Then we think of the New Testament apostles and all the redeemed throughout 2,000 years of church history—heaven will be the home for all of them. Unfortunately, however, the vast majority of the world's population will not be there. Heaven, as Christ explained, is a special place for special people.

Perhaps you think that you might be lost in the crowd, or you are afraid you'll get stuck on the 1,000th floor when all of the activity is in the downstairs lounge! No worry. If heaven does literally have the length and width given in the Bible, we will be able to travel in a moment of time, just as Christ did after His resurrection. All you will have to do is *think about where you'd like to be* and you'll be there! Everyone will be equally important; we will all be given individualized attention. As someone has said, there will be a crown awaiting us that no one else can wear; a dwelling place that no one else can enter.

Are you weary of moving around the country? Some families move every two years. Wives don't know whether they should unpack or not. It's too hot in Arizona, too cold in Chicago, and too rainy in Seattle. But when you arrive in heaven, you can unpack. It's your final home.

■ A Special Person

A special place, yes. But our focus in heaven will be on the Special Person, Christ. "And if I go and prepare a place for you, I will come again and receive you to Myself; that where I am there you may be also" (v. 3). Those are the words the disciples wanted to hear. Heaven is the place where all human needs for fellowship and security are fully met.

When Christ said that He will return, it is probably best to understand this as a reference to His return to earth. Though that event is still future, the bodies of the disciples themselves shall be resurrected at the rapture, and the disciples, together with us, will rejoice with the Lord in the air. His return is explained more fully in passages such as 1 Thessalonians 4:13-18 and 1 Corinthians 15:50-58.

As children, we probably thought that heaven might be boring—one eternal church service. You begin on page one of the hymnal and sing your way through. No matter how exciting it may be at the beginning, it's got to eventually become monotonous. Someone has said that the popular conception is that heaven would be like spending a rainy weekend at camp! You may have heard the story of a preacher who asked all those who wanted to go to heaven to raise their hands. All hands shot up, except that of a man sitting in the front seat. "Don't you want to go to heaven?" the preacher asked. "Sure," he said, "but I thought you were getting a group together to go right now!"

Heaven means the personal presence of Christ and the splendor of God the Father. Every church on earth has its faults. All of us worship imperfectly; our theology is not always as accurate as it should be. We sometimes don't get along with each other, and even have harsh words between us.

But in heaven we will be in a state of perfection. We will worship God the Father and God the Son. Our anxieties will be over forever; God will be dwelling with His people, and He shall wipe away all tears from our eyes. All negative emotions will vanish, and there will be no trace of sorrow or its effects. We'll walk and worship with the King. Someone has written:

Just think of stepping on shore
And finding it heaven,
Of taking hold of a hand
And finding it God's,
Of breathing new air
And finding it celestial,
Of waking up in glory
And finding it home!

■ A Special Relationship

Walk through a hospital today, and you will find bodies that are deteriorating. A young woman is dying of cancer; a middle-age man is struggling with heart disease, his wife and children bent over him in quiet anxiety. An accident victim is rushed through the hallway, his face disfigured.

Now visualize heaven: new bodies not subject to disease, pain, or old age—that's what we have waiting for us. A body that can travel through space and that needs no sleep.

Will a baby still be a baby in heaven? No, physically we will all be like Christ. Those who are deformed in this life will most assuredly be without defect in the life to come. The resurrection body will be created out of preexisting materials, but will not be limited by present handicaps (1 Cor. 15:42-44).

Yes, you will still be the same person in heaven. Your mind, with all of its history and memories, will be a part of that new body. The real you will be fully present.

Will we know each other in heaven? Of course. On the Mount of Transfiguration, Peter, James, and John knew Moses and Elijah. I doubt whether they had to be formally introduced. We'll likely have an intuition or instant knowledge of one another. Not omniscience, but very active and bright minds.

Will your mother still be your mother in heaven? Yes, we will know each other for who we were on earth. But there will be a difference: rather than being a member of a small family, you will be a member of an extended family. The same affection and love you have for your family on earth will be extended to the larger family of God. No one will feel alienated; no problem with rejection or inferiority. One family, with Christ being accessible to all.

This knowledge sustained the disciples in the moment of distress. Knowing that they would eventually be with Christ would help them through the period of separation and sorrow. They could have a calm heart though sailing a stormy sea.

■ A Special Way

Thomas was confused. Christ was talking about going to the Father's house and returning. He assured the disciples that they also knew the way. After all, He had frequently spoken to them about His impending death and the salvation it would bring.

But Thomas wasn't so sure he knew. Or more accurately, he was sure he didn't know, so he asked, "Lord, we do not know where You are going; how do we know the way?" (v. 5) In answer to his specific question, Christ gives one of His famous "I Am" pronouncements. Read it carefully: "I am the way, and the truth, and the life; no one comes to the Father, but through Me" (v. 6).

The way. Christ is the route to God the Father and to the heavenly city He had just been talking about. He is the beginning and the end of our journey.

Consider the alcoholic, defiled by sensual living and looking for "a way out." He does not have to make his own path; there is one that is already made. Christ is the way to a new kind of life, ready to lead men and women to God.

He is also the *end* of the journey. Christ knows the Father; indeed, He said to Philip, "He that hath seen Me hath seen the Father" (v. 9). You don't have to know everything about the trip as long as you have a reliable guide. We've all been lost in a strange city, and when asking for directions, have heard, "Sorry, I'm new here too!" What a difference when you are with someone who knows the whole trip from beginning to end!

One a day a tourist walking across a desert asked a guide, "Where is the path?" to which the guide replied, "I am the path." Someone has said that Christ is the way from the place of man's ruin all the way to God the Father; all the way from the city of destruction to the heavenly city.

If you are not fussy about your destination, then the road you take does not matter much. In fact, if you don't know where you are going, any path will get you there.

Christ is both the travel agent and the means of transportation. He is the One who takes bookings for heaven. He has the ability to bring the most unworthy sinners to God. Yes, He is the *way*.

Christ is also the *truth*. He is the essence of all truth—truth which exists objectively and eternally.

Years ago, a Christian student I knew sat next to a bitter atheist in a university classroom. This young foe of Christianity wrote a ten-page paper which derided Christianity for its belief in truth. His bottom line: there is no truth; thus Christ was wrong in claiming to have some! When the Christian woman who sat next to him gave me a copy of the paper, I wrote a short reply. I pointed out that if there is no such thing as truth, then we could discard his ten-page paper immediately—obviously it contained no truth! In fact, I challenged him to be consistent: he should never speak again, because whenever he did, we would know in advance that what he was saying could not be true! After he read my reply, he did not speak to the Christian girl for the rest of the semester.

The world says there is no truth, but Christ is the One who claims to be truth. He is both consistent and reliable. He is a dependable source of revelation. Even the psalmist recognized that truth resides in God. "Teach me Thy way, O Lord; I will walk in Thy truth; unite my heart to fear Thy name" (Ps. 86:11).

Christ's consistency between life and lip should not go unnoticed. In some cases, the character of a man might not have direct bearing on what he teaches. But think of the inconsistency of a greedy man pleading for generosity, or a bitter man waxing eloquent on the need for forgiveness and love. In teachings regarding moral and spiritual issues, we expect the teacher to practice what he preaches. Christ did.

Jesus explained to His followers, "You shall know the truth, and the truth shall make you free" (John 8:32). Truth is liberating because we are beset with falsehoods; we are by nature prone to accept the lies of the devil. Truth leads to victory.

What does it mean for Christ to be the *life?* He has resources for those who see the insufficiency of their own strength. He can give life and give it more abundantly.

Christ may be thinking about physical life, but more importantly, He is speaking about spiritual life—that is, bringing believers into direct contact with the Father. The world speaks about "living it up," but actually, sensual pleasure is nothing more than a slow form of spiritual death; it is "living it down." Christ said, "The thief comes only to steal, and kill, and destroy; I came that they might have life, and might have it abundantly" (John 10:10).

Christ is the way, the truth, and the life, and, therefore, He adds, "No one comes to the Father but through Me" (v. 6). This clear statement of the exclusivity of the Gospel message shows the complete uniqueness of Jesus Christ. Thomas had said that he did not know the way. But if he knew Christ, he did know the way after all. The way to heaven is so narrow that even some who cast out demons in Christ's name will miss the entrance. It's not the way of the proud or the so-called broadminded. It's the way of the cross, the way of faith and repentance. Someone has said, "Without the way there is no going; without the truth there is no knowing; without the life there is no living."

■ A Special Response

What was the effect of all this on the disciples? They could rest in the confidence that Christ's departure would not be permanent. He had gone to heaven but would come again to receive them. They were on the right road; they were on the side of truth and blessed with eternal life.

Such knowledge would give the disciples the confidence needed to transfer the ownership of their lives to God. They could make heavenly investments that would eventually greet them in the life beyond. They could be different from the man who entered heaven and was surprised to find that he was not given a beautiful home, but just a comfortable apartment. When he voiced a complaint, he was told, "This is the best we could do with what you sent up here." This fictitious story is a poignant reminder that what we hold to ourselves, we shall lose forever, and what we give to Christ we shall meet again.

These are matters that would concern the disciples at some later date. For now, they rested in the assurance that their separation from Christ would be temporary. The troubled waters were calmed by the soothing words of

Christ's promises. They believed in God, and they could also believe in Him. No matter how many storms they would encounter, their sail was set to make it to the other side.

Many people live their lives crucified between two thieves—the regrets of yesterday and the anxieties of tomorrow. In washing the disciples' feet, Christ illustrated how He could wipe out the regrets of yesterday. In talking confidently about heaven, He proved His ability to rid them of the anxieties of tomorrow. They could endure the separation and fear much better because of the assurance that everything would end all right.

In a World War II prison camp, shouts of joy broke out one morning amid the smell of disease and death. The emaciated prisoners, though weak from starvation and suffering, found cause to laugh. What could possibly induce elation in the face of depression and hopelessness? One of the prisoners had an old transistor radio and that morning heard the news that the war was over. Though their circumstances had not changed, the prisoners could now endure the suffering, because they were confident that freedom lay just around the corner.

Our problems become lighter when we weigh them against our final triumph in heaven. A few days, months, or even years of affliction cannot be compared with eternity. "For momentary, light affliction is producing for us an eternal weight of glory far beyond all comparison, while we look not at the things which are seen, but at the things which are not seen; for the things which are seen are temporal, but the things which are not seen are eternal" (2 Cor. 4:17-18).

Yes, many storms awaited the disciples. But they were relieved to know that their safety to the other side was guaranteed. They could set their sail toward heaven regardless of the direction of the winds of hostility and misunderstanding.

A person with a whole heart is calm in the storm. For it's not the direction of the wind, but the setting of the sail, that determines your destination. No matter how far you venture out on the sea, your heart need never leave the port.

Gazing at the promises and glancing at the waves is God's way of keeping us calm until we reach the other side.

CHAPTER 3

NURTURING A PRAYING HEART

JOHN 14:8-15

During World War II, bombers destroyed a church in Berlin. As the rubble was cleared away, workers found a statue of Christ with the hands missing. A sculptor agreed to restore the structure, but the church leaders decided to keep it as it was, as a vivid reminder that *we are Christ's hands.*

While other men's work is interrupted by death, Christ told the disciples that His work was to continue after His departure. His deeds would be reproduced and perpetuated without much interruption.

The disciples were hardly ready for such an awesome responsibility. To take over after Christ was gone was like a midget trying to fill the shoes of a giant. How could their work be even a pale copy of the miraculous ministry of Christ?

Christ would give them some pointed teaching about their resources. But first, Thomas and Philip had some questions that needed to be answered. Thomas had told Christ that he did not know where the Lord was going, nor did he know the way. Christ explained that He is the way, and then added, "If you had known Me, you would have known My Father also; from now on you know Him, and have seen Him" (John 14:7).

This statement evoked a question from Philip, who wanted a more detailed revelation of the Father. "Lord, show us the Father and it is enough for us" (v. 8). We commend Philip for his desire to seek God. Apparently, he was expecting a theophany such as those given during Old Testament times. But to this statement, Jesus gives a startling reply. "Have I been so long with you, and yet you have not come to know Me, Philip? He who has seen Me has seen the Father; how do you say, 'Show us the Father'? (v. 9)

Christ affirms the unbreakable unity between God the Father and God the Son. To see Him is to see the Father; indeed, the very words that Christ speaks are spoken by the Father's initiative.

Knowing that Christ was a man, yet simultaneously believing He was God, was difficult for the disciples to accept. The most important commandment was, "You shall have no other gods before Me" (Ex. 20:3). The fundamental affirmation in Judaism was, "Hear, O Israel! The Lord is our God, the Lord is one" (Deut. 6:4). The concept of the Trinity had simply not occurred to the disciples. They knew it was blasphemy for a man to claim to be God—yet, this Man made such claims repeatedly. That's why they were so puzzled when Christ said, "He that hath seen Me hath seen the Father."

Now Christ gave them words that would both inspire and awe them at the same time. In His absence, His work would be carried on by the handful of disciples He had trained. His work would not be interrupted by His departure. To raise the level of the disciples' understanding of their role, our Lord said, "Truly, truly, I say to you, he who believes in Me, the works that I do shall he do also; and greater works than these shall He do; because I go to the Father. And whatever you ask in My name, that will I do, that the Father may be glorified in the Son. If you ask Me anything in My name, I will do it" (vv. 12-14).

Imagine the startled looks on the faces of the disciples when Christ gave three promises: (1) They would do the *same* works as He; (2) they would do *greater* works; and (3) whatever they asked in His name, they would receive.

What did Christ mean? Should His words be taken literally? If so, what is the link that ties His power to our performance?

■ Greater Works

To do the *same* works as Christ was breathtaking enough. The New Testament biographies of Jesus tell of thrilling miracles: people were healed of incurable diseases, storms were calmed, and bread multiplied in the hands of the disciples so that more than 5,000 people were fed with a boy's lunch. Then if that were not enough, demons were cast out and the dead were raised! Someone has said that our Lord passed through the land as a river of life. Before Him were hopeless sufferers, but after He walked by, there was healing and hope.

Yet, Christ said His followers would do the *same* works. This was literally fulfilled in the Book of Acts when the apostles did the works of Christ. "And also the people from the cities in the vicinity of Jerusalem were coming together, bringing people who were sick or afflicted with unclean spirits; and they were all being healed" (Acts 5:16). Yes, the apostles even raised the dead! But after that period of church history, the miracles tapered off and occurred only sporadically as the centuries unfolded.

If we are surprised by the promise of Christ, "The works that I do, you shall do also," we are even more startled by a second category of works that He refers to: "Greater works than these shall he do; because I go to the Father" (v. 12). Even the disciples in the Book of Acts did not do greater miracles than those of Christ. Faith healers today, even if found to be authentic, do not dwarf the miracles on the pages of the New Testament.

That's why many Bible scholars see in this prediction a reference to the worldwide impact of the Gospel spread by believers throughout the centuries. The works of Christ from heaven, done through multiplied thousands of His followers, would be greater in two ways.

First, they are greater in kind. The skin of the leper whom Christ healed would again be wrinkled with age; Lazarus would have to die again. But when a sinner is turned from his ways, it results in everlasting life. It's been said that eternity is greater than time just as the ocean is greater than a creek. The pain from which salvation delivers men is greater than that which a disease could ever inflict. As F.B. Meyer wrote, "The soul is greater than the body, as the jewel than the casket. All work, therefore, which produces as great an effect on the soul-life as miracles on the physical life, must be proportionately greater, as the tenant is greater than the house, as the immortal than the mortal."[1]

The miracles brought about by the Gospel are also greater in *extent*—that is, evangelization takes place around the world. Christ essentially stayed within the borders of what we call Israel. The geographical scope of His ministry was incredibly small, perhaps 100 miles from north to south and 40 miles east to west. All that He had to show for His ministry was the 120 in the Upper Room gathered after His ascension. But the disciples and their followers would carry the Good News up and down the highways of Asia Minor and eventually across the seas to other parts of Europe and finally the world. The power of the Gospel would not be stopped by invading armies. It was not helpless against the powerful political forces that would be hostile to its basic premises. The mighty Roman Empire would be permanently changed by the impact of the message.

What is more, Christ spoke only Greek and Aramic. His ministry was so limited that David Hume, the famous agnostic, said that it was immoral for God to expect the whole world to believe a revelation that was limited to such a small area of the world, given in such a short span of time, and in only one culture. But through the work of the disciples, the message of Christ would eventually get to every country of the world. A stone was thrown into the pond and its ripples would be felt on every shoreline.

Today, thanks to such organizations as Wycliffe Bible Translators, the Bible is available in more languages than is any other book. Millions of believers live in hostile regimes, such as China and Russia, but even there the church that Christ founded continues to grow.

A soul claimed for eternity is of more value than a thousand physical healings that can never permanently stave off death. Those who are co-laborers with Christ have indeed done greater works than He. Christ's work through His followers is greater than that which He did as one Person walking the streets of Jerusalem or the shores of Galilee.

Whereas the Gospels record the works of Christ on earth, the Book of Acts and the pages of church history detail the works of Christ as He is seated in heaven. The reason He coul tell His followers that they could expect to do "greater works" was because He was going to the

Father. They would have the privilege of serving Christ after the Cross and the Ascension. The act of redemption would soon be in the past; they then could proclaim the Good News with confidence. And the resources associated with the completed work of Christ would give them the impetus to evangelize the world. Rather than two hands, now there would be thousands, all taking their direction from the Head in heaven.

■ A Greater Promise

In the same breath, Christ adds a sweeping promise regarding prayer. "And whatever you ask in My name, that I will do, that the Father may be glorified in the Son. If you ask Me anything in My name, I will do it" (vv. 13-14).

On the surface, at least, this statement appears to be untrue. We can all think of requests that have gone unanswered. And here, Christ seems to be giving the disciples a *carte blanche*—anything they request, they will receive.

Some have suggested that these words apply only to the apostles and not to their followers. In the church age, following the death and resurrection of Christ, Paul, who gave much instruction about prayer, never mentions such a general promise. Rather, he exhorts us, "Be anxious for nothing, but in everything by prayer and supplication with thanksgiving, let your requests be made known to God. And the peace of God, which surpasses all comprehension, shall guard your hearts and minds in Christ Jesus" (Phil. 4:6-7). He gives no promise that our requests will be fulfilled, but just that we will have the peace of Christ and the ability to accept whatever Christ gives us.

The other way to interpret Christ's words is to notice that there are several restrictions that limit the scope of the promise. First, Christ says whatever you ask "in My name." That means the request must be consistent with the character of Christ. To do something in the name of another is to act as his representative. As an ambassador speaks in the name of a king, so we must be subject to the will and purposes of Christ.

Occasionally, I've been asked to lend my name to an organization to help it receive recognition or credibility. I'm much more careful than I used to be, because at least once I let my name be identified with a group that did not live up to my expectations. I've determined to have my name linked only with those whose beliefs and stated goals are consistent with mine.

Christ doesn't lend His good name to just anyone. Of course, some take it to themselves without His approval. They even do miracles in His name, yet eventually are disqualified from eternal life. But to pray in the name of Christ means that we live near enough to Him that we ask those petitions that He would desire. As F.B. Meyer says, "Let the living water, which has descended from the eternal city return back to its source through the channel of your heart. This is praying in His name and according to His nature."[2]

Second, Christ says that we should ask "that the Father may be glorified in the Son." Our prayers must be subject to the will, approval, and glorification of God. In fact, that's the way the Father evaluates everything—does it glorify His name or does it not? God is particularly concerned about His glory, and whether or not His name is honored.

The main purpose of prayer is not to get us out of bankruptcy or to lessen the pain of an inflated tumor. God is interested in these problems and often does do just as we ask. But His primary purpose goes beyond our immediate needs. It is His glory that is of primary importance.

Prayer in the name of Christ and for the glory of God is difficult. It excludes our selfishness, our own temporal perspective, and it forces us to trust the wisdom of God. But when the character of God, and the purposes of God come together, we know the request will be granted.

To understand this more clearly, let us consider the example of Christ. We all know that He lived for the glory of God. "I glorified Thee on the earth, having accomplished the work which Thou hast given Me to do" (John 17:4). He lived to please the Father, and God was glorified at Christ's expense. To unfold the plan of God, to reveal the Father to men—that was Christ's bread and butter. To this day, His cherished purpose is to make the Father loved and adored.

Christ met all of the requirements for effective prayer. In fact, there is no prayer that He ever uttered that was not fully answered. He, above all, teaches us what it is to pray for the glory of God. Note carefully: Christ did not use prayer as a means to rid Himself of the physical and emotional pain of Gethsemane and the cross. The closest He ever came to asking the Father to exempt Him from the torture that lay before Him was when He said, "My Father, if it is possible, let this cup pass from Me; yet, not as I will, but as Thou wilt" (Matt. 26:39). But when He prayed a second time, His will was now resolute and, in wholehearted submission, He said, "My Father, if this cannot pass away unless I drink it, Thy will be done" (Matt. 26:42). *Prayer was the means He used to gather His strength to go through with His assignment; it was not the means of delivering Him from it.* Prayer is not always a substitute for pain; sometimes it is the preparation for it!

Some people try prayer just once, like the little girl who prayed earnestly that the doll she held in her hand would become a real baby. When the anticipated miracle didn't happen, she became so disillusioned that she didn't pray for several years. But prayer is not asking for what we want; it is developing trust that can handle those moments when there is no miracle and when life itself seems to fall apart. Look at Christ in Gethsemane, filled with emotional turbulence, yet submissive to the relentless pain that He would endure on the cross.

Prayer is not like putting a quarter into a slot machine—a gambler is willing to part with a bit of money hoping the return might be worthwhile. When nothing comes out, he looks for some other quick fix that appears to have a better chance of success. In contrast, prayer is hard work; it is getting to know God well enough that we can discern His mind and intentions. And in those instances where we are baffled, the Holy Spirit comes to our aid and through us prays with groanings that cannot be put into human words.

■ A Greater Challenge

The need of the hour is for prayer, but this alarm sounded by so many falls on deaf ears. Why don't we pray more when we know we should? Marriages are falling apart; tragedies happen in rapid succession. And many believers have no victory at all over these circumstances. A visitor from another planet would never guess that we had secret resources that are unavailable to the general population. We live in an age when we need to see miracles—lives put together, individuals saved, and strong, self-centered wills broken before the Lord. So why don't we pray more?

Most of us remember George Mueller as a man who founded several orphanages and sustained them without asking for funds. But according to his testimony, he did not do this primarily for the benefit of bereft children, but to demonstrate that God, even in his day, could still answer prayer.

There were three categories of believers who troubled Mueller. First, there were those of old age who feared that their savings would not sustain them until the end. They lived with the anxiety of anticipating life in the poorhouse. When he spoke to them about faith in God, they countered by saying that God no longer did miracles in our day.

Second, there were Christian businessmen who felt they had to carry on their transactions in the same way the unconverted did. They expressed a wish to be different but contended that the competition was such that they could not be expected to make money if they did not operate on the same basis as the world.

Third, there were those who continued in doubtful professions, but feared to resign lest they should not be able to get another position elsewhere.

Rather than lecture on prayer, Mueller decided he wanted to strengthen their faith by showing that God was completely trustworthy. He would begin an orphanage with this simple rule: he would never let its financial needs be made known. As God supplied, by one miracle after another, even the skeptical would have to admit that the living God was as good as His word.

In his book *Answers to Prayer*, Mueller tells the story of one miracle after another. Children were ready to sit down to eat, not knowing that there was no food in the house; but after prayer was said, there was a knock on the door with a meal adequate for all of them! Sometimes God seemed to let him dangle out on a limb and would come and rescue him and the children in the nick of time. He also learned the folly of trusting other human beings. One day, a rich man told Mueller that a considerable sum of money would soon be given to him based on an impending business deal. He promised he would give it to the orphanage. But though the needs of the orphanage increased, the money never came. God taught Mueller to value such promises as nothing, and that "the mind ought never to be directed toward them, but to the living God."[3] Once his trust was directed to God alone, the man who made the promise sent the money!

Mueller urged believers not to think of him as an extraordinary believer who had privileges that others lacked. No, he was just taking the promises of Christ seriously and invited other believers to test the reliablity of God.

Notice that Mueller's first objective was the glory of God—that was even more important than the orphans. Yes, the glory of God must supercede the temporal needs of life. Second, he prayed in the name of Christ, consistent with the character of our Saviour. And he persisted in that praying regardless of how God tested him, that he might still see the miracles of the Lord.

That statue of Christ without hands in a church in Berlin, indeed, packs a powerful message. The Saviour is gone, but His work goes on uninterrupted. The two hands of the Man of Galilee are exchanged for the tens of thousands of hands of His followers who go throughout the world proclaiming the Gospel of Christ. Rather than having the eyes of the blind opened, the eyes of the soul would be opened to the reality of Christ's message. And so, Christ, the Head, directs His followers from heaven as they do greater works than He.

Greater works, greater promises, and a greater example—all these were given to the disciples that evening. Although the look of Calvary was already on the face of our Lord, He knew that when it was over, His disciples would carry on. With such an arsenal of promises, they would soon be ready to take on the world.

Friedrich Nietzche, the atheistic German philosopher, made this surly remark to some Christians one day: "If you want me to believe in your Redeemer, then you've got to look more redeemed."

In His prayer, Christ wanted us to be like Him in our character and in our works too. The redeemed should emulate the Redeemer. Prayer is the link between His power and our performance. One praying heart can make other hearts whole.

NOTES

1. Meyer, F.B., *Expositions of John, XIII-XXI* (New York: Fleming H. Revell, 1898), p. 59.
2. Ibid., p. 128.
3. Mueller, George, *Answers to Prayer* (Chicago: Moody Press), p. 26.

CHAPTER 4

DEVELOPING A COURAGEOUS HEART

JOHN 14:16-31

It's frightening to walk alone into unprotected darkness. How much better to be with someone who has the ability to protect you from the hazards of the unknown path; somebody who promises *he will be with you no matter what.*

For three years, the disciples could depend on Jesus for everything. He would still the storm on Galilee, multiply food, and answer His critics with logic and wit. It was easy to be Christ's disciples standing next to Him; they could weather many blows with the strong Son of God at their side.

But now they would be alone. Jesus would not be there to talk with; He would not be there to bail them out of a mess. It's not just that they'd miss His friendship; they would be without the intense moral and spiritual strength His presence generated. Already they were beginning to feel like orphans. Lonely, weak, and without direction. And those feelings made them vulnerable to the world. So Christ gave them some welcome reassurance. "I will not leave you as orphans. I will come to you" (John 14:18).

In our society, parents have been known to abandon their children. New mothers have left their babies in alleys or on doorsteps, or even walked away from older children at home. In contrast, Christ doesn't abandon His children. When you're a member of His family, you'll never be an orphan; you'll never be lost in a child custody battle. In fact, Christ is saying to His disciples, *"I'll be closer to you than ever before!"*

Specifically, the Holy Spirit was given to take the place of the physical presence of Christ in our lives. When Jesus says, "And I will ask the Father, and He will give you another Helper, that He may be with you forever" (v. 16), we should notice that in Greek there are two words for *another.* One definition means "similar"; another means "identical." It's the second word that Christ uses here. "When I leave you, I am sending One who is identical to Me to take My place," He is saying.

We often exalt the privileges of the early disciples who personally walked with Christ. We think of how great it would have been if we had been on the Sea of Galilee when Jesus calmed the storm; or how thrilling if we had been one of the disciples when He fed the multitude. Tourists who go to Israel today often want to find some place where they can say with authority, "I stood exactly where Christ stood." We are absorbed by the thought that He actually was on this earth, and we would like to be able to identify with that experience. But surprisingly, Jesus said, "It is to your advantage if I go away" (16:7). The gift of the Holy Spirit multiplies His presence in the life of every believer. When Christ was here on earth, He could not be in Galilee and Jerusalem at the same time. But by means of the Holy Spirit, Christ can now be with every individual believer in any part of the world. The Holy Spirit enables Christ to be with all believers simultaneously. Our problem is that we confuse "bodily" with "real." Of course, Christ's body was real—but the Holy Spirit is not "less real" because He is invisible. In fact, through the gift of the Spirit, Christ is even nearer to us than He was to the disciples 2,000 years ago. Sometimes they had to be separated from Him. We are *never* separated.

Of course, when we speak about the coming of the Holy Spirit, let us remember that in one sense He has always been in the world. After all, the Holy Spirit is God. Yet, the Spirit came on the Day of Pentecost in a special way, and for a specific purpose. Just as God the Father was on Mount Sinai before He appeared to Moses, so the Holy Spirit has been in the world before He came to indwell individual believers.

Let me emphasize that the Holy Spirit is a Person. Have you ever tried to play chess with a computer? You can receive some satisfaction when you beat the machine. Even though you may feel great about winning, the computer isn't at all concerned. It has the advantage of never being discouraged because of defeat, but it also is never elated because of victory. The only emotion involved in the game is what *you* bring it. It's not too helpful if you live in a lonely apartment.

A second level of interaction can take place with an animal. Those of you who have become fond of a dog or cat know how much you can get attached to such creatures. Yet, animals can never take the place of another human being.

We reserve the word *personality* to refer to people, or other intelligent beings. Beings that can communicate on our level—mind, emotion, and will. That is precisely what the Holy Spirit is: a Person who has a mind, emotions, and will. He is just as real as any friend you may have.

What special duties did Christ assign to the Holy Spirit?

What does He delight to do in the lives of God's people?

■ A Living Helper

Once again, consider Christ's promise in verse 16: "And I will ask the Father, and He will give you another Helper, that He may be with you forever." That word *helper* is sometimes translated "comforter" or "counselor" and also "advocate." Literally, it means "one who is called alongside to help." Perhaps the ambiguity of the word emphasizes that the Holy Spirit helps us in many different ways. It's not just that He consoles us in our sorrow, but He also makes us strong in the face of opposition.

Christ would not have placed the tremendous responsibility of world evangelism on the shoulders of the disciples unless He had compensated for their weaknesses. And it is the Holy Spirit who gives us both boldness and strength to do the will of God. The disorganized, weak-willed disciples were changed into a world-conquering fellowship. When the Holy Spirit came, power came to the church.

As an advocate, the Spirit defends us against the attacks of Satan. When we find it difficult to pray, He "intercedes for us with groanings too deep for words" (Rom. 8:26). Though He convicts us of sin, He does not accuse us. He becomes whatever we need at the moment to live a successful Christian life.

I repeat: the gift of the Holy Spirit is given as a substitute for the physical presence of Christ in our lives. What did Christ do for His disciples when He was on earth? He calmed storms, provided food, and gave them comfort when they needed it. And that's precisely why the Holy Spirit has been given to us. And fortunately, greater is He that is in us than he that is in the world.

Alexander Maclaren, in stressing the Holy Spirit's continuation of Christ's ministry, points out that the Holy Spirit is really like Christ "so all that that handful of men found of sweetness and shelter and assured guidance, and stay for their weakness, and enlightenment for their darkness, and companionship for their solitude, and a breast on which to rest their heads, and love in which to bathe their hearts—all *these* this divine Spirit will bring to each of us if we will."[1] There you have it: the Holy Spirit being whatever we need moment by moment. He is the Helper called alongside so that we might not walk alone through the valleys and dark nights of our experience.

■ A Living Companion

Jesus said of the Holy Spirit, "That is the Spirit of Truth, whom the world cannot receive, because it does not behold Him or know Him, but you know Him because He abides with you, and will be in you" (v. 17). Here, Christ, in a single statement, differentiates between the work of the Holy Spirit in the Old Testament and the New Testament Eras. The Spirit was *with* the disciples but after He came at Pentecost, He would be *in* the disciples. Although some people in the Old Testament enjoyed the indwelling of the Spirit, their numbers were limited. Only a few had this blessing.

Frequently, in the Old Testament, it is said that the Holy Spirit "came upon a person." This indicates the temporary character of the Holy Spirit's ministry in the lives of Old Testament saints. Furthermore, today, those who are indwelt by the Spirit enjoy this blessing forever (14:16). The Holy Spirit isn't simply close to us, but actually *in* us. He is an abiding guest.

Later, Christ said, "If anyone loves Me, he will keep My word; and My Father will love him, and We will come to him, and make Our abode with Him" (v. 23). Interestingly, the only other place that this word *abode* is found in the New Testament is in verse 2 where it is translated "dwelling places" ("mansions," KJV). God the Father and God the Son take up residence in the bodies of those who are born again. As Meyer wrote, "God is willing to become the mansion of the soul that believes in Christ, but asks in return that such a one should prepare a guest-chamber and become a mansion in which He may dwell. As He steals with noiseless tread into the loving, believing heart, I hear Him say, 'This is My rest forever; here will I dwell, for I have desired it.' "[2]

That God should be willing to indwell our bodies with our limitations and sinfulness is proof of the amazing condescension of God! We stand amazed, not that He pities our race, but that He should love us as He loves His Son and that both the Father and the Son should abide within us is really more that we can understand. He does not indwell unbelievers, for Christ says that the Comforter cannot be received by the world.

God has always wanted a dwelling place on the earth. In the Old Testament, the temple area had a courtyard and then in the inner sanctuary was the holy of holies where the Shekinah Glory came. Yet, today, God does not dwell there. In 1 Corinthians, Paul says, "Or do you not know that your body is the temple of the Holy Spirit who is in you, whom you have from God, and that you are not your own?" (6:19) One Greek word for temple refers to the outer courtyard; another Greek word means the inner shrine, or the holy of holies. When Paul says "Your body is the *temple* of the Holy Spirit," he uses the second word which specifically refers to the place where God dwells. This means that God's presence which is no longer in the physical temple in Jerusalem has been moved into the body of every Christian.

A mother told her daughter that she should not bring a trashy novel into the church building. This woman, like many today, apparently thought that the sanctuary of God was the church building. But actually, it is our physical body. *We* are the shrine where God dwells. If we have reading material that should not be brought into the church building, it most certainly should be burned. Nothing should defile the place where God really lives—namely, the bodies of believers.

Just think of the implications. Christ is closer than a friend who is at your elbow looking over your shoulder. When you take the subway, He goes with you. When you walk down the street, He is there; if you sin, He must suffer through the entire experience. For the Holy Spirit does not leave the sinning Christian, but is grieved through such disobedience. The Spirit, who thinks, feels, and knows, experiences hurt. "And do not grieve the Holy Spirit of God, by whom you were sealed for the day of redemption" (Eph. 4:30). His companionship is as real as taking a shopping trip with your favorite friend.

■ A Living Teacher

Not only do we receive a helper and companion, but we also have a living Teacher. Christ says, "These things I have spoken to you, while abiding with you. But the Helper, the Holy Spirit, whom the Father will send in My name, He will teach you all things, and bring to your remembrance all that I said unto you" (14:25-26). He is the Spirit of Truth, and He delights to bring the revelation of truth to our hearts. A wise teacher doesn't overwhelm his pupils with an avalanche of facts that they cannot grasp, but leads them step by step as they are able to follow the information. Christ knew that He had so much more to say, but the disciples weren't ready for it.

But later, the Holy Spirit would guide them. Luther said, "The simple maid studying the Bible with the help of the Holy Spirit's grasp is better than the greatest scholar studying without the help of the Holy Spirit." We've all met people who can't seem to grasp even the most elementary spiritual truth. What is more, the human mind tends to distort spiritual reality unless it is clarified by the illuminating ministry of the Holy Spirit. The Spirit constantly points to Christ, and helps us in our struggles for truth.

The mind, of course, is a great battleground for truth or error. In one of his books, missionary Don Richardson tells the story of how a tribe was unable to memorize Scripture. Whenever they got home from their Sunday services, they could not remember what they had learned. The missionaries got together and bound Satan's power, since Christ says it is he who snatches the seed of the Word of God from the human mind (Mark 4:15). After Satan was rebuked, the congregation's memory quickened, and they were able to learn and grasp spiritual truth as never before. The Spirit is a teacher who guides men and women to truth.

There was a guide who was known for his ability to go through the desert and never be lost. He didn't carry a compass, but he did have a homing pigeon with a string on its leg. When the guide was confused, he put the bird in the air, and it circled for a few moments, then headed toward home. At that point the man would bring the bird back, knowing what direction he should be taking. In the same way, God has given us the Holy Spirit who always points in the direction of Christ and home. He's our helper, companion, and teacher who keeps clarifying our relationship with Christ. And, of course, He is our guide who is with us each step of the way.

■ A Well of Water

Many Christians know about the coming of the Holy Spirit, but they are confused about how to walk in the Spirit. For many it seems like an impossible dream. But actually, every believer, regardless of how young in the Lord, has the privilege of walking in the Spirit.

In John 7:37, Jesus stood and cried, "If any man is thirsty, let him come to Me and drink. He who believes in Me, as the Scripture said, 'From his innermost being shall flow rivers of living water.'" But this He spoke of the Spirit whom those who believed in Him were to receive; for the Spirit was not yet given because Jesus was not yet glorified (7:37-39).

Usually teachers sat, but Christ became impatient, rose, and called out to the huge crowd. Someone has said that His voice was "as loud as thunder, as sweet as music, and as piercing as agony." He disrupted the activity of the feast because He knew that many were dissatisfied with superficial observances. At least some were spiritually thirsty.

We can't fully appreciate the ministry of the Holy Spirit as long as we are temporarily satisfied with the watering holes of the world. Pleasure, success, fame, and love ... these tend to fill in the voids of our lives. If someone gets a promotion, he is often less inclined to rely on the Holy Spirit. Whenever life itself gives us thrills, it's hard to hear Christ's voice. But notice the promise; *we can have an endless supply of living water!*

On what *basis* does Christ offer water for thirsty souls? It's the ascension that gives Him the right to make such a promise. Before Christ's glorification to heaven, He could not have given the Comforter, the Holy Spirit. But because He has ascended, the Holy Spirit can be poured out in a new way. Let me explain it this way: the death of

Christ obtained our forgiveness, but the ascension of Christ is the basis of the Holy Spirit's coming. Let's suppose that you were to buy a book that came in two volumes. If, after you returned home, you discovered that you had brought only one volume from the bookstore, you would return the next day to pick up the second volume. There would be no additional charge because it was already included in the original price. Many Christians know only about the one volume—the forgiveness of sins. They know little about the privilege of walking in the Spirit; they don't understand that daily living water is available from the Spirit who indwells them.

And who qualifies for the refreshing water that Christ spoke about? He replies, "The thirsty." You don't have to be a supersaint to know the blessing of the Holy Spirit. Let's not think that walking in the Spirit is a reward for spiritual service. Some believers strive and agonize thinking that the blessings of the Holy Spirit are dependent upon their own efforts. But like the horse straining vainly for the carrot dangling in front of it, they never get what they seek. The filling of the Spirit always eludes them; no matter how active they may be, it seems to escape their grasp.

A minister friend told me how he wept at many altars seeking the filling of the Holy Spirit, but he would always leave empty, unsure as to whether or not he found what he sought. As far as he knew, he was meeting all of the requirements, but left thirsty. Why? He still had not seen that the filling of the Holy Spirit is received by faith.

Let's suppose you led someone to Christ, and the person prayed, "O Lord, I pray that you might save me." Such a person has not yet come to full assurance. How much better if he were to pray, "Lord, I thank You that You *have* saved me and received me." Walking in the

Spirit involves the same kind of faith. It's saying to the Lord, "I thank You that I have received the Holy Spirit in my heart and now, in faith, I want to begin to walk in His power."

The famous preacher F.B. Meyer told about his experience: "I left the prayer meeting and crept away into the lane praying, 'O Lord, if there was ever a man who needs the power of the Holy Spirit it is I. But I do not know how to receive Him; I am too tired, too worn, too nervously run down to agonize.' Then a voice said to me, 'As you took forgiveness from the hand of the dying Christ, take the Holy Spirit from the hand of the living Christ.' " Meyer said that he then took for the first time and has been taking every since!

Walking in the Spirit implies that we take a step at a time. As a child often fails when learning to walk, so we learn amid many failures and few successes. If you, by an act of faith, receive the fullness of the Spirit, how long will it last? I don't know. How long did the last drink of water you took last before you became thirsty? Just as we must drink water several times a day, so we must receive from the ascended Christ the strength of the Holy Spirit hour by hour. When D.L. Moody was asked why he had to be filled with the Holy Spirit so often, he replied in characteristic bluntness, "Because I leak."

Christ offered living water to the woman at the well. She was interested in finding a well of water within her springing up into everlasting life because she had a series of bad marriages and at the time was living with a man who was not her husband. She could not look to her husband for spiritual strength; she needed inner resources that were independent of the circumstances that were around her.

As we practice walking in the Spirit, we will become

Christ-conscious. We'll remember that wherever we go, we take Christ with us. Whether in church, or in sinful temptations, He is with us all the time. Also, we must become sin-conscious. That is, we must keep current accounts with God. As soon as the Holy Spirit points out sin in our lives, we must be willing to confess it and forsake it. Many Christians become disappointed by looking within and seeing all the sin that is there. So they experience remorse, which is nothing more than facing sin apart from the sight of Jesus! Through many failures and few successes, we will soon learn to walk and find that Christ's promises are not extravagant—the Holy Spirit is indeed a companion qualified to substitute for the physical presence of Christ in our lives.

A.J. Gordon, one of the founders of Gordon Divinity School, looked across a field and saw what he believed to be a man pumping water. He couldn't believe that this man could pump water so consistently, and with such power, without getting tired. After Dr. Gordon walked across the field, he discovered what he saw was not an actual man but a figure painted to look like a man. In fact, this figure wasn't pumping water at all—it was set up mechanically in such a way that an artesian well was doing the pumping! The wooden figure was doing nothing but responding to the power of the water and was being propelled by the strength of this natural spring.

Wouldn't it be wonderful if there was some way that we, instead of striving in the Christian life, could find the strength and power to strive against sin and win the battles that we often lose? Wouldn't it be a relief to have an artesian well gushing up every single day of our lives?

That is precisely what Christ promised. A helper, a companion, a teacher, and a source of flowing, refreshing water. It's ours to be received by faith.

With such a supply of energy, the disciples were more prepared to face the dark nights ahead of them. Their fearful hearts were strengthened when they heard that Christ would still be with them in the person of the Holy Spirit.

Christ by His Spirit is with us. Courage does not depend on who you are but who is standing beside you.

NOTES

1. Maclaren, Alexander, *With Christ in the Upper Room* (Grand Rapids: Baker Book House, 1956), p. 84.
2. Meyer, *Expositions*, p. 96.

CHAPTER 5

SUSTAINING A JOYFUL HEART

JOHN 15:1-11

Perhaps you've heard of the gifted speaker who said that his most difficult speaking assignment was an address given to the National Conference of Undertakers titled "How to Look Sad at a Ten-Thousand-Dollar Funeral."

But an even more difficult assignment would be to speak on the topic: "How to Teach the Early Christians to Be Sad." Though their enemies tried to put a lid on their joy, it just bubbled up again and again.

Henry Wingblade used to say that Christian personality is hidden deep inside us. It is unseen, like the soup carried in a tureen high over a waiter's head. No one knows what is inside unless the waiter is bumped or trips.

When a disciple of Christ is bumped, joy should spill out. After all, Christ promised a constant supply of joy for all those who believe in Him.

The world says that joy can be found through a change in circumstances: take a vacation, earn more money, spend more money, or save more. Or even more popular today is the notion that we should change ourselves. Self-help books tell us to "discover the new you," and be enlightened regarding the resources that are already latent in every human being.

Jesus has a different formula for joy. "These things I have spoken to you, that My joy may be in you, and that your joy may be full" (John 15:11). Most of us don't have enough joy for ourselves, much less enough to share with someone else. "Some Christians are like a cup half filled, trying desperately to spill over," a friend of mine said. But Jesus said it is possible to have enough joy for yourself and still enough to share.

What is the source of joy Christ talks about? It's learning to abide in Christ so that we become fruit-bearing Christians. Let's consider some of the relationships given in the popular metaphor of the vine and the branches.

■ Joy Depends on Fruitfulness

When Jesus said, "These things I have spoken unto you," He was talking about becoming a fruit-bearing disciple. What is fruitfulness? It's the outward expression of the inner nature. Some people can walk through a forest and identify the kinds of trees just by looking at the bark and the leaves. I can't do that. But if I see some oranges growing on a tree, it does not take me long to conclude that I must be looking at an orange tree. There's an outward expression of the inner nature.

The fruit of Christ's life in us is, therefore, the outer expression of His inner power. Fruit isn't just other Christians. No, it's the inner nature of Christ that eventually will bring about the new birth in the lives of others. Fruit is the product of what God can do and not what you and I can manufacture.

Christ said, "I am the true Vine, and My Father is the Vinedresser. Every branch in Me that does not bear fruit,

He takes away; and every branch that bears fruit, He prunes it, that it may bear more fruit" (vv. 1-2). The Father has a knife that cuts and He uses it to make us more fruitful. Grape growers cut back young branches so they will expend their energy in becoming more firmly entrenched in the vine. Just so, God the Father cuts the leaves away so that we might become even more fruitful.

When you look at a vineyard just after the branches have been cut back, it looks as if the vinedresser has been absolutely ruthless. Scattered on the ground are bright green leaves, and bare stems almost appear to be bleeding from the sharp knife. To the untrained eye, it seems wasteful; but not one stroke was done at random. As one writer said, "There was nothing cut away which it was not loss to keep and gain to lose; and it was all done artistically, scientifically, for a set purpose—that the plant might bring forth more fruit."[1]

And how does the Father cut back the branches? He uses the Word of God and the circumstances of life. "You are already clean because of the Word which I have spoken unto You" (v. 3). If we allow the Word to prune us, some of the bitter chastisement that we experience from time to time might be needless. To quote Spurgeon, "The Word is often the knife with which the great Husbandman prunes the vine; and, brothers and sisters, if we were more willing to feel the edge of the Word, and to let it cut away even something that may be very dear to us, we should not need so much pruning by affliction. It is because that first knife does not always produce the desired result that another sharp tool is used by which we are effectually pruned."[2]

And what about those branches that don't bear fruit? There are several different explanations for the branches that are taken away and burned in the fire. Some teach that they represent the unconverted who make professions of faith but are not genuinely joined to Christ. Like Judas, who appeared to be like the other disciples, these people have never been converted. God eventually removes such branches from the vine and burns them.

There's no doubt that some people only appear to be converted, but their relationship with Christ is only superficial. They are parasites on the vine and will be eventually removed. To men they appear as part of the true vine, but God knows they have never been connected. They await the fire of hell.

A second interpretation says that this passage teaches that true believers (i.e. those who are genuinely "in Christ") can eventually be lost. Although these branches are at one time "in Christ," they are at a later time separated from Christ and burned. This interpretation, however, is difficult to reconcile with other passages in John's Gospel that teach unequivocally that Christ loses none of His sheep. "My sheep hear My voice, and I know them, and they follow Me; and I give eternal life to them, and they shall never perish; and no one shall snatch them out of My hand" (John 10:27-28).

A third view is that these branches represent genuine Christians, but they are removed by God's discipline because of carnality and disobedience. Yet, they do not lose their salvation; the fire spoken of is not hell, but the fire at the Judgment Seat of Jesus Christ when some believers' lives will be consumed, yet they shall be "saved so as by fire."

Regardless of how we understand the worthless branches, we cannot lose sight of Christ's central point: *as far as God is concerned, there is no reason for you to live, except to bear fruit.* If you are not fruitful, God says you are worthless. The text talks about "fruit," but also "more fruit," and again Christ speaks of "much fruit." God is concerned about one thing in your life—fruitfulness. Since the wood of the branches of grapes is worthless, it is simply taken and burned. If you thought the purpose of your life was to earn a decent living, you are wrong. Or if you thought the reason for your existence was tied to your own happiness and personal fulfillment, you are wrong again. *Fruit bearing* is God's single overriding concern for you. And if you don't bear fruit, you are worthless to Him.

■ Fruitfulness Is Dependent on Relationship

Jesus said, "Abide in Me, and I in you. As the branch cannot bear fruit of itself, unless it abides in the vine, so neither can you, unless you abide in Me" (v. 4). The key to fruit bearing is relationship—it's depending on the life of the vine. To put it clearly: it is not the responsibility of the branch to bear fruit, the responsibility rests with the vine. A branch, as someone has said, it just a grape rack—just a vehicle of the vine's life.

Think of the close relationship between Christ and His people. Though a vast gulf separates us from Christ so far as our natures are concerned, yet Christ joins Himself to us! The life of the branch and the life of the vine are one. There is only one stream of sap, one essential life-giving energy that pervades all of the branches regardless of where they may eventually grow and find themselves. And as already emphasized, it's the responsibility of the vine to provide everything that is needed for the branch to bear fruit.

Let's suppose you lead someone to Christ. Who gets the credit? Of course, we know that Christ receives the glory, for He alone can beget life. But now let's suppose that you have prayed, you are filled with the Holy Spirit, and you share the same Gospel with another person. Is it your fault that they do not believe? Of course, Christ hasn't failed, but it is His responsibility and not ours to bring about eternal life. Whatever God's ultimate purpose in the life of that individual is, the fact is that it is up to God, and not us, to grant men and women the gift of eternal life. What I am saying is this: if you have prayed and are submitted to the leadership of Christ and you present the Gospel, He must be the one to bear fruit; we of ourselves cannot. This frees us in our witnessing, because we realize that responsibility rests with the vine and not the branch.

And precisely how much can the branch do without the vine? Nothing! Christians who concentrate on good works, rather than their relationship with Christ are missing the point Christ is teaching here. It's not a matter of *what* we do, but a matter of who works through us, that determines whether we are fruit-bearing Christians or not. John MacArthur writes, "Even strong branches cannot bear fruit independent of the vine. Cut off from the vine, even the strongest branches become as helpless as the weakest; the most beautiful are as helpless as the ugliest; and the best are as worthless as the worst."[3] That's why learning to abide is absolutely essential in our quest to please God. Whatever we do independently of Christ is just so much deadwood. God will use His sharp knife until we bleed, so that our worthless deeds are laid bare. We will stand before Him impoverished, so that we might learn once for all the need to receive our strength and motivation from Christ alone. Are we willing to pray, "Lord, cut me if only my fruit for You might increase."

Andrew Murray emphasized that there is a big difference between work and fruit in the Christian life. A machine can do *work;* only life can bear *fruit.* A law can force one to work; only life can spontaneously bring forth fruit.

■ Your Relationship Depends on Abiding

What does it mean to abide in Christ? It's hard to improve on the definition of Godet: "It is the continuous act by which the Christian lays aside all he might draw from his own wisdom, strength and merit, to desire all from Christ by the inward aspiration of faith."

Perhaps the best way to understand what abiding in Christ means is to grasp Christ's relationship to the Father: "If you keep My commandments, you will abide in My love; just as I have kept My Father's commandments and abide in His love" (v. 10). Repeatedly, Christ said, "I do nothing of Myself." In the manner that Christ did nothing apart from the strength of His Father, so we can do nothing apart from Him. The same dependence, faith, and humility that characterized Christ must be ours as well.

But how do we strengthen that relationship with Christ so that we can bear much fruit? To abide in Christ means "to dwell." It means that He is the very air we breathe and the world we live in. He becomes the focus of our thoughts. It involves yieldedness, availability in prayer, and actually praying. For if we abide in Him, we shall ask what we will and it shall be done unto us.

But how can we abide amid the pressures of life? There are so many interruptions and irritations that edge us away from Christ. We may begin well at the start of the day but by midmorning abiding is far from our minds. Let me quote at length from the experience of Hudson Taylor:

> I knew that if only I could abide in Christ all would be well, but I could not. I would begin the day with prayer, determined not to take my eye off Him for a moment, but the pressure of duties, sometimes very trying, and

constant interruptions apt to be so wearying, cause me to forget Him.

There was nothing so much I desired as holiness, nothing I so much needed; but far from it in any measure, attaining it, the more I strove after it, the more it eluded my grasp, until hope itself almost died out, and I began to think that—perhaps to make heaven the sweeter, God would not give it down here. . . . I strove for faith, but it would not come; I tried to exercise it, but in vain. Seeing more and more wondrous supply of grace laid up in Jesus, the fullness of our precious Saviour, my guilt and helplessness seemed to increase.

How shall I get my faith strengthened? Then the Lord showed me the truth of our oneness with Jesus as I had never known it before. My faith could be strengthened not by striving after faith, but by resting on the Faithful One. "Ah, there is rest," I thought. "I have striven in vain to rest in Him. I'll strive no more. For has not He promised to abide with me, never to leave me, never to fail me?"

Nor was this all He showed me, nor one half. As I thought of the vine and the branches, what light the Blessed Spirit poured direct into my soul! How great seemed my mistake in wishing to get the sap, the fullness out of Him! I saw not only that Jesus will never leave me, but I am a member of His body, of His flesh, and of His bones. The vine is not the root merely, but all the root, the stem, the branches, twigs, leaves, flowers, and fruit. And Jesus is not that alone—He is soil and sunshine, air and showers, and ten thousand times more than we ever dreamed, wished, or needed.

The sweetest part is the rest which full identification brings. I am no longer anxious about anything, as I realize this; for He, I know, is able to carry out His will and His will is mine.[4]

Hudson Taylor discovered that he was indeed already in Christ, but he had to simply rest in the sufficient Saviour. His experience, though dramatic, can be ours if we remember that abiding is not dependent upon our feelings, or the mood we happen to be in at the moment. It's a matter of faith. Even in the most trying circumstances we can focus our mind on Christ and be strengthened by knowing that we are one with him, sharing His life and experiencing His grace.

■ Abiding Results in Blessing

When you become a fruit-bearing Christian, you inherit many blessings. First, you experience answered prayer. "If you abide in me and My words abide in you, ask whatever you wish, and it shall be done for you" (v. 7). Christ speaks here of a reciprocal relationship: we abide in Him, and His words abide in us.

We all struggle with such a sweeping promise but must realize that a person who carefully abides in Christ will always ask according to the will of God (as we noted in chapter 3). We must see His mind and delight ourselves in His purposes. As Hudson Taylor said, "His will is mine."

Second, we will experience fulfillment and joy. Christ said, "These things I have spoken unto you . . . that your joy may be full" (v. 11). This statement stands in contrast to many Christians whose lives are filled with complaining and bitterness. The focus of their attention is circumstances, not the pure and trustworthy words of Christ. For Christ promises joy in the midst of the hardships of life. As Don Carson, Trinity Evangelical Divinity School professor, said, "The joy Jesus promises is not some cheap glow dependent on outward circumstances."[5]

Abiding in Christ releases the fruit of the Spirit in our lives—love, joy, and peace, to name a few. It's a life of intimacy that gives the power of Christ the opportunity of expressing itself through individual believers.

Joy, then, is a by-product of living as a fruitful Christian. It's not to be sought directly but is the outgrowth of a personal, living relationship with Christ.

Remember, if you aren't a fruit-bearing Christian, though God loves you, He considers you to be worthless. The branches that do not bear fruit are considered as common garbage; those that bear at least some fruit are pruned to bear even more.

We must give up our quest for joy and concentrate on fruit bearing. The more fruitfulness, the more joy. It's just as simple and profound as that. C.S. Lewis says, "The ultimate purpose of God in all His work is to increase joy."

Joy is the ointment that can heal a fractured heart. Christ gives it to those who draw their spiritual strength from Him.

NOTES

1. Maclaren, *With Christ*, p. 172.
2. Spurgeon, Charles H., *Spurgeon's Expository Encyclopedia*, *vol. 4* (Grand Rapids: Baker Book House, 1977), p. 337.
   Quoted in *The Legacy of Jesus* by John MacArthur, Jr. (Chicago: Moody Press, 1986), p. 105.
3. Ibid., p. 110.
4. Taylor, Dr. & Mrs. Howard, *Hudson Taylor's Spiritual Secret* (Chicago: Moody Press, 1932), pp. 158-161.
5. Carson, D.A., *The Farewell Discourse and Final Prayer of Jesus* (Grand Rapids: Baker Book House, 1980), p. 100.

CHAPTER 6

MAINTAINING A CARING HEART

JOHN 15:12-17

A famous British actor left a suicide note which read, "I'm taking the only way out of this hell of loneliness." Loneliness doesn't exist only in the world, but it is found within the church too. Consider the words of one older woman: "I sit in the pew next to a warm body every week, but I feel no heat. I'm in the faith, but I draw no active love. I sing the hymns with those next to me, but I hear only my own voice. When the service is finished, I leave as I came in—hungry for someone to touch me, to tell me that I'm a person worth something to somebody. Just a smile would do it, or perhaps some gesture, some sign that I am not a stranger."

No one can live happily without friends. Those who find friendships difficult often isolate themselves from those who would be their friends. If you've been hurt in the past, you might be afraid to risk a close relationship again. Yet we all need friends, and they need us. As Mary Hughes put it, "A friend is the first person who comes in when the whole world has gone out."

Friends are necessary, not just for emotional support, but also because there are some responsibilities we simply cannot handle alone. Somewhere I read this humorous account of what happened when a bricklayer tried to do the job on his own:

Dear Sir:
I am writing in response to your request for more information concerning Block #11 on the insurance form which asks for "cause of injuries" wherein I put "Trying to do the job alone." You said you needed more information so I trust the following will be sufficient.

I am a bricklayer by trade and on the date of injuries I was working alone laying brick around the top of a four-story building when I realized that I had about 500 pounds of brick left over. Rather than carry the bricks down by hand, I decided to put them into a barrel and lower them by a pulley which was fastened to the top of the building. I secured the end of the rope at ground level and went up to the top of the building and loaded the bricks into the barrel and swung the barrel out with the bricks in it. I then went down and untied the rope, holding it securely to insure the slow descent of the barrel.

As you will note on Block #6 of the insurance form, I weigh 145 pounds. But to my shock at being jerked off the ground so quickly, I lost my presence of mind and forgot to let go of the rope. Between the second and third floors I met the barrel coming down. This accounts for the bruises and lacerations on my upper body.

Regaining my presence of mind again, I held tightly to the rope and proceeded rapidly up the side of the building, not stopping until my right hand was jammed in the pulley. This accounts for the broken thumb.

Despite the pain, I retained my presence of mind and held tightly to the rope. At approximately the same time, however, the barrel of bricks hit the ground and the bottom fell out of the barrel. Devoid of the weight of the bricks, the barrel then weighed 50 pounds. I again refer you to Block #6 and my weight.

As you would guess, I began a rapid descent. In the vicinity of the second floor I met the barrel coming up. This explains the injuries to my legs and lower body. Slowed only slightly, I continued my descent, landing on the pile of bricks. This accounts for my sprained back and internal injuries.

I am sorry to report, however, that at this point, I again lost my presence of mind and let go of the rope, and as you can imagine, the empty barrel crashed down on me. This accounts for my head injuries.

I trust this answers your concern. Please know that I am finished "trying to do the job alone."

God never intended that we "do the job alone." If we want to have a whole heart in a broken world, we need close friends who can help us in our struggles and rejoice in our victories. An active alcoholic isn't helped by another active alcoholic; a thief will not come clean when he is in the company of thieves. We can scarcely exaggerate the benefits of a good friend who will lift us up rather than drag us down.

Jesus, on the eve of His crucifixion, elevated His disciples to the stature of friends. We choose our friends on the basis of compatibility, whether they have the same interests as we do. Or perhaps we are attracted by their personality. But Christ made friends by winning His enemies over. When we were without strength, in due time Christ died for the ungodly. More than 100 years ago, poet Edwin Markham described the determined power of love in winning an enemy over.

> He drew a circle and left me out,
> A heretic, a rebel, a thing to flout.
> But love and I had the will to win;
> We drew a circle and took him in!

Christ drew a circle that included His disciples and us as well. Think of the honor of being chosen to be the friend of a monarch! Powerful leaders often have many acquaintances but few friends. As one wealthy man put it, "People always want to see me to get something. . . . Nobody cares about me as a person." But here, Christ invites us to the inner circle. It's not just that we come because we need Him—there's a sense in which He needs us as well!

We should be surprised that Christ is not afraid to be so closely identified with His people. Though we are fundamentally distinct from the God-Man, yet He embraces us. We will never understand the gulf Christ bridged when he called us His friends. His holiness does not cause Him to withdraw into isolation away from sinful humanity, but because of His impending death, He is able to reach out and bring His followers into the family. Elsewhere, we read, "He is not ashamed to call them brethren" (Heb. 2:11). One day, when there was a discussion about the identity of Christ's brothers, the Lord answered, " 'Who is my mother and who are My brothers?' And stretching out His hand toward the disciples, He said, 'Behold My mother and My brothers! For whoever shall do the will of My Father who is in heaven, he is My brother and sister and mother' " (Matt. 12:48-50).

Friends, brothers—these are words that Christ used to identify His true followers. Someone has said of Him, "The Prince makes a friend of the beggar."

We've all had the experience of being criticized for befriending someone of doubtful reputation. Christ was ridiculed on earth for eating with publicans and sinners. And even God has been accused of impropriety because of His close associations with sinful humanity. A society for the spread of atheism issued a leaflet that mocked God because of His close relationship with old Testament heroes. The tract correctly noted that Abraham lied, being willing to sacrifice the honor of his wife, Sarah, to save his own skin. Yet, it was pointed out that Abraham was called "a friend of God." Jacob was a cheater, and yet in the Bible he is also called "a prince with God." Moses was a murderer, and yet God used him to give the Ten Commandments, one of which said, "Thou shalt not kill." The atheists pointed out that Moses was a hypocrite, preaching a message that he himself did not live up to. David was correctly identified as one who had committed adultery and murder, and yet the Bible speaks of him as "a man after God's own heart."

In their own perverse way, the atheists were right in asking, *What kind of a God would associate with these people?*" And when we see the weaknesses of the disciples, we might also ask what kind of a Saviour would call these men, with all of their failings, His friends!

The answer, of course, is that Christ would soon give His life as a sacrifice for sin. As a result, God would maintain His honor and, at the same time, justify sinners. Therefore, Christ can be perfectly exonorated in calling His disciples "friends." Despite their imperfections, His grace could reach across the infinite chasm between the holy God and sinful man.

> What a friend we have in Jesus,
> All our sins and griefs to bear!
> What a privilege to carry
> Everything to God in prayer!

What are some of the characteristics of friendship with Christ? We do have a name to live up to. But fortunately, Christ gives us the resources to be credible members of His special circle of friends.

■ The Badge of Friendship Is Love

"This is My commandment, that you love one another, just as I have loved you. Greater love has no man than this, that one lay down his life for his friends" (vv. 12-13). Here, Christ gave the world the right to judge whether or not we were His followers by our love for one another. "By this all men will know that you are My disciples, if you have love for one another" (John 13:35). Our assignment is to love one another as He loved us.

What kind of love did He display? Christ was obedient in saving us regardless of the cost. He came down from heaven not to do His own will, but the will of the Father who sent Him. It was a costly love, and one that He expects to reproduce in us. Someone said, "I asked Jesus how much He loved me. He stretched out His arms and said, 'This much,' and died." He loved us so much that He died for us.

To love one another is not Christ's suggestion, but His *commandment*. We might think it inconsistent for Him to command us to love. Love, we are told, cannot be turned on or off like a water faucet. But we must come back to the biblical conception of love: it is an act of the will by which we choose to be sacrificially involved in the lives of others. In fact, we cannot really say that we love someone until we have made some sacrifices in his/her favor.

There are three kinds of love: *eros* is sexual love that often takes but never gives. *Phileo* is affection that gives and takes. *Agape* is a love that gives and then gives some more even when there is no return. Four-year-old Linda, hugging a doll in each of her pudgy little arms, understood agape love when she said, "Momma, I love them, and love them, and love them, but they never love me back." And when asked why she loved the ugly, ragged doll the most, she said, "If I didn't love her, who would?"

Calvary was less than twenty-four hours away when Jesus said we are to love one another as He loved us. No man can have greater love for another than to lay down his life for a friend. In his novel *A Tale of Two Cities*, Charles Dickens tells of a young Englishman who was caught trying to flee France with his family during the French Revolution. Because of the French hatred for the English, the young man was sentenced to death on the guillotine. An hour before his execution, a guard and a French friend visited him. After the guard left, the friend ordered the doomed man to exchange clothes with him. "I cannot do it," the Englishman protested. "You must," he said. "Your wife and child are waiting for you in a carriage at the door." Moments later, the guard came, and unknowingly escorted the Englishman safely to his waiting family. An hour later, the Frenchman was executed in his friend's place.

Christ calls us to strong friendships. Yet, how easily our relationships are broken when they become demanding or when we are asked to become sacrificial. But the better we are friends with Christ, the easier it will be to love God's difficult children. Tertullian, a leader of the early church, when speaking about the impact of the church in the world in his era, said, "It is our care for the helpless, our practice of loving-kindness, that brands us in the eyes of many of our opponents. 'Look!' they say, 'How they love one another! Look how they are prepared to die for one another.' "

Let's not confuse love with sympathy. We can sympathize with people who are starving in another country, but we cannot say we love them until we have been sacrificially involved in their need. Christ can say authoritatively that He loves us because He laid down His life on our behalf.

There is, of course, a condition for our friendship with Christ. "You are My friends, if you do what I command you" (15:14). This should dispel the notion that our friendship is on an equal basis. Christ stresses two ideas that are not incompatible: submission and friendship. When we submit to Him, we are His friends. And obedience first and foremost demands that we love one another.

Why not thank God for that person He has brought into your life whom you are finding difficult to love? If love were easy, it could hardly be the badge of friendship. It's because it is difficult that our credentials as Christ's friends really mean something to other believers and the world. Why should we accept an easy mark of friendship when Christ so clearly spells out a more difficult one? A false friend, it has been said, is like your shadow. As long as there is sunshine, he sticks by. But the minute you step into the shade, he disappears. We are Christ's friends, and He stays with us no matter what.

■ The Reward of Friendship Is Intimacy

"No longer do I call you slaves; for the slave does not know what his master is doing; but I have called you friends, for all things that I have heard from My Father I have made known to you" (15:15). A slave does what he is told, whether he understands the purpose of his work or not. Slaves were often seen as tools to achieve the aims of someone else. Often they were not considered intelligent enough to appreciate what their master was planning. Thinking of life as we know it today, imagine working in an automobile factory, and being responsible to tighten just one bolt in each passing car without ever seeing the end product. Rote obedience, without any understanding of ultimate purposes, is slavery indeed.

That's why Jesus told His disciples that He no longer thought of them as slaves, but as friends. The distinction is one of intimacy. Slaves were not permitted to eat at the same table as their masters. Often slaves had separate quarters and were never invited to participate in family discussions. But Jesus now has drawn a circle to include us; He invites us to His table so we can share family matters.

A king would be insulted if his waiter asked questions about the details of his personal life or responsibilities in the kingdom. Yet a close friend could ask the king some questions and not be out of place. Over a period of years, I have befriended a man who is notoriously difficult to "get next to," as the expression goes. Yet, because of our friendship, I have earned the right to ask him about his troubled marriage.

It's friendship that makes the difference. Christ told His friends everything He wished to. But, of course, what He shared was limited by His own purposes and by their own ability to understand. Today we wish He had told them much more. A bereaved mother would like to ask Him about the destiny of little children who have yet not known enough to believe in Him. All of us would like to know why God allows children to starve when some rain sent to parched ground could alleviate the suffering. The problem of human need vexes us, and God's purposes are often shrouded in mystery.

As Alexander Maclaren said, it would have been easy for God to have lifted a little corner of the veil and let more of the light shine out. Why does He open one finger instead of the whole palm? Maclaren answers, "Because He loves . . . and for all of the gaps that are left, let us bow quietly and believe that if it had been better for us, He would have spoken. 'If it were not so, I would have told you.' 'Trust Me! I tell you all that is good for you to receive.' "[1] And perhaps if we were silent we could hear more. "If we silenced our passion, ambition, and selfishness . . . if we withdrew ourselves, as we ought to do, from the babel of the world, and hid ourselves in His pavilion from the strife of tongues; if we took less of our religion out of books and from other people, and were more accustomed to 'dwell in the secret place of the Most High' and to say, 'Speak, Friend, for Thy friend heareth'; we should more often understand how real today is the voice of Christ to them that love him."[2]

Friends enjoy secrets. In Psalm 103:7, we read, "He made known His ways unto Moses; His acts unto the Children of Israel." The Children of Israel saw only miraculous intervention, but only Moses was permitted to speak face to face with God as a man speaks with his friend. Yet, today, because of Christ, we stand nearer to God than Moses did at the door of the tabernacle or on Mount Sinai when he beheld God face to face! It is to such intimacy that Christ calls us.

David understood that special relationship with God. "The secret of the Lord is for those who fear Him, and He will make them know His covenant" (Ps. 25:14). My wife and I received a letter from a teenage girl who had been experiencing emotional turbulence because of difficult problems in her home. She wrote, "I like to tell my problems to Jesus because He doesn't tell anyone else what I say to Him." Here was a young girl who discovered that Christ is a friend to be trusted. He is a friend who will never betray us. Furthermore, He is not far off; He need not be called into our living room or closet but is always available. Blessed are those who have special secrets with Christ who invites us to call ourselves His friends.

George Elliot said, "O the comfort, the inexpressible comfort of feeling safe with a person, having neither to weigh thoughts or measure words, but to pour them all out just as they are, chaff and grain together, knowing that a faithful hand will take and sift them, keep what is worth keeping and then, with a breath of kindness, blow the rest away." Christ invites us to that kind of intimacy.

Do you feel comfortable in Christ's presence? If our Lord seems distant, it's not because He is trying to play hide-and-seek. He's waiting for us to make some hard choices that will make friendship with Him a priority.

■ The Basis of Friendship Is Christ's Choice

Just when Christ gave the disciples some teaching that might cause them to fall into pride, He often tempered His remarks by reminding them that their relationship was based on His choice, not theirs. "You did not choose Me, but I chose you, and appointed you, that you should go and bear fruit, and that your fruit should remain; that whatever you ask of the Father in My name, He may give it to you" (John 15:16). Friends must be chosen. And Christ made it clear that He chose the disciples to bear fruit and not vice versa. Often new believers, in giving expression to their faith, will say, "I found Christ as my

Saviour." Though such language is understandable, the reverse is actually true: *Christ found us.* Our choice of Him is but a response to His initiative and work. We can't take credit for our salvation. "We love Him because He first loved us." As the songwriter put it:

> I sought the Lord, and afterward I knew,
> He moved my soul to seek Him, seeking me:
> It was not I that found, O Saviour true;
> No, I was found of Thee.

Christ chose us for the purpose of doing His work on earth and to bear fruit, a kind of fruit that would remain. Nothing perishes more quickly than fruit, even if it is kept cool and dry. Yet, Christ says that we can bear a different kind of fruit that will withstand the test of ages. We can serve God in such a way that what we do will last forever.

Recently, I spoke with a man who is bitter at God because he is going blind. He says that in the past he was "a self-made man." Now he's been humbled, unable to do countless things that he once did. His ministry is over, and he sees no reason to continue to live. Yet every believer has the ability to bear fruit even if it is simply to be faithful in obscurity. Some people have the privilege of bearing fruit out in the open where others can watch; others bear fruit in the shade. And, of course, as we know, it takes more of the life and the power of Christ to be faithful in the invisible matters than it does in the visible ones. Regardless of our lot in life, we can bear fruit if we serve the Lord in joy and faith.

■ The Development of Friendship Is Growth

Friendship takes time and involves trust. Many believers are acquainted with Christ; they may say good morning to

Him and even good night, but there is no intimacy. Their walk with the Saviour is stale and forced. Yet Christ stands ready to help us develop a friendship that will become enjoyable and even delightful. "In Thy presence is fullness of joy; at Thy right hand there are pleasures forevermore" (Psalm 16:11, KJV).

What does it take to develop friendship with Christ? First, there is *time*. The world is constantly competing for our affections. And yet, to be a friend of the world is to be an enemy of God. The fact is, we cannot have dual friendship—either it will be Christ or it will be our own plans, desires, and appetites. Since a good friendship will always be tested, God tests us by bringing pressures into our lives that will force us to make some hard choices. One of those decisions is the matter of quality time in the presence of God. It's impossible to live a successful Christian life without meditation in the Word and prayer—and for most of us it must be done before 9 A.M. That sets the tone for communication with Christ for the rest of the day. But we will never spend quality time with Christ unless we resist the other voices that call to us, begging for attention and involvement.

Friendship with Christ is not a once-a-week arrangement, but a daily relationship where sacrificial choices must be made in Christ's favor. The use of our time separates the sheep from the goats. Here we can distinguish between those who want the benefits of Christ's friendship without the effort to cultivate the relationship.

Then there is *trust*. Most of us think that friendship with Christ is impractical because it involves a relationship with an unseen Being. So God sends difficulties into our lives to give us opportunities to share our burden with the One who elevates us to the status of friends. Yet, so often we balk at the opportunity to trust Christ in the little matters of life as well as the big ones. The trust we exercised at the time of salvation must be extended to every area of our lives. If we can entrust the destiny of our souls to this Friend, why do we find it so hard to give Him the details of our schedules, problems, and difficulties? *Trust* must be developed or else we cannot claim intimate friendship with our Lord.

Finally, there are *trials*. That's where growth in trust takes place—it's when we find ourselves without any recourse except to appeal to Christ, the Lord. Barbara Martin wrote an article about the difficulties her grandparents had in the Great Depression of the 1930s. In midwinter, her grandfather had been injured in a coal mine accident and was unable to work for many weeks. The food supply nearly disappeared and they knew no one who could help them. One morning, as the grandmother watched her offspring devour their breakfast biscuits, she calculated how many more days it would be before the flour would be gone, and no food would be left in the house. "O God," she murmured, "must I watch my children starve?"

That day, she didn't say the blessing and when reminded of it, they bowed their heads and Grandma recited, "God is great. God is good. And we thank Him for this—" The prayer she had quoted every day for years stuck in her throat. As she looked at the faces of her hungry children, she cried out, "I'm not thankful, and I will not lie to You any longer, God!" The children were astonished as tears streaked down Grandma's face. "How can I be thankful when my children suffer? Don't You hear the growls of their empty bellies? You gave these children to me. Help me feed them!"

With that Grandma snatched her coat from the wall and slammed out the door. She ran from the house, trying to escape the pale, thin faces she had left behind. She tripped and fell into the snow where she lay still, feeling too weary to rise. Through the tears that blurred her vision, her eyes slowly focused on something on the ground a few feet from where she lay. Incredulously, she realized she had literally stumbled upon a twenty-dollar bill. With that, she went to the grocery store and came back loaded with food. Barbara ends by saying, "Years later, as Grandma told the story, her eyes glistened with emotion. 'I have never prayed a more urgent prayer,' she said, 'and I have never received a more glorious reply.'"

Who can deny that Christ did a miracle for a friend? There is, after all, a Friend who sticks closer than a brother, and He was there in the time of need. As we draw near to Him, He draws nearer to us.

You may remember the story of the couple who was driving through a beautiful wooded area. The woman said to her husband, "Years ago, when we drove through such beautiful scenery, we sat close and held hands." The man looked at her through the corner of his eye and said, "Remember, I haven't moved."

Have you?

NOTES

1. Maclaren, *With Christ*, p. 216.
2. Ibid., p. 217.

CHAPTER 7

ACCEPTING A PERSECUTED HEART

JOHN 15:18-27; 16:1-4

If you were to stand on a street corner in Chicago, or any other American city, and ask, "What do you think of Christ?" most people would say that He was a teacher, a leader, or one who displayed loving concern for people.

Laudable as those answers may seem, they are actually an insult to Christ. If that's all He was, He was a liar.

Remember this basic axiom: *The better the world understands the biblical Christ, the more the world hates Him.* If they speak well of Him, it's because they don't understand Him. The secular musicals, movies, and books that are favorable to Christ inevitably misunderstand His message and work on earth. To quote one writer, "What we believe to be precious it [the world] regards as of no account. What we believe to be fundamental truth, it passes by as of little importance. Much which we feel to be wrong, it regards as good. Our tools are its tinsel, and its jewels are our tinsel."[1]

Christ and the world represent two conflicting philosophies that have no common ground between them. By *world* I am, of course, referring to greedy materialism, selfishness, and the pursuit of illicit pleasures. John defined it as "the lust of the flesh and the lust of the eyes and the boastful pride of life," going on to say that it "is not from the Father, but is from the world. And the world is passing away and also its lusts; but the one who does the will of God abides forever" (1 John 2:16-17). This world system is diametrically opposed to Christ. If you have any doubt about whether the world opposes Christ, watch a few hours of prime-time TV. You'll see that the values promoted are contrary to the purity and righteousness that Christ taught. In fact, some television programs are deliberately designed to break down our resistance to incest, immorality, and homosexuality. That is the world that stands in opposition to Christ.

If you want to have a whole heart in a broken world, you will have to accept the antagonism of the world system. In fact, the more outspoken you are with your faith, the more the world will oppose you. At root is the conflict between Satan and God. As F.B. Meyer wrote, "Between such irreconcilable opposites as the church and the world, there cannot but be antagonism and strife. Each treasures and seeks what the other rejects as worthless. Each is devoted to ends that are inimical to the dearest interests of the others."[2]

Christ has just told the disciples about their new status as His friends. He explained the special relationship of the true Vine and the branches; the disciples know that they are precious to the Saviour. But now is the time to explain the darker side of commitment to Christ. Someone has said that Christ never hid His scars to win a disciple. Just as He went the way of agony and humiliation, so the disciples must follow.

The clearer the line between us and the world, the more

antagonism we will attract. What response can we expect from the world? Jesus gives us several.

■ Hated by the World

Christ commands the disciples to love one another, not only because love is of God, but because they will need each other's strength to combat the world system. "If the world hates you, you know that it has hated Me before it hated you. If you are of the world, the world would love its own; but because you are not of the world, but I chose you out of the world, therefore the world hates you" (John 15:18-19). The world hates a nonconformist—especially one who brings sin out into the open.

Christ was hated because He exposed the world. When light comes, the darkness does not receive it. The world does not mind religion as long as it appeals to pride and self-effort; but the world becomes antagonistic when Jesus Christ penetrates beneath the outer shell and exposes the inner world of humanity. Someone has said that Jesus is so pure that dirty men either get cleaned up or else they must loathe purity. And, of course, as His followers pursue righteousness, people of the world will despise their friendship. In the manner of Cain, who killed Abel "because his deeds were evil, and his brother's were righteous" (1 John 3:12), so the world hates to be next to someone who is a true follower of Jesus Christ.

Liars do not like friends who speak only the truth; alcoholics are bothered by those who do not have to drink; the man who swears feels uncomfortable in the presence of a Christian who speaks wholesome words. Standing before Christ, we cannot hold our heads high with pride, but rather we must kneel to receive His mercy and salvation.

Christ was hated by the world because He made the

religious leaders look bad. He spoke with authority, He had insight into human nature, and He did not flatter His listeners with pious words about human good. He talked about the sinfulness of the heart, and judged the hidden motives of the pious. His followers, if they are indeed His disciples, must do the same.

What is more, Christ judges the world. "If I had not come and spoken to them, they would not have sin, but now they have no excuse for their sin" (v. 22). Jesus is not saying that men would have been innocent if He had not come. The world was already sinful and rebellious before He appeared in the manger at Bethlehem. Christ's coming highlighted sin in human hearts: He pointed it out so people had less grounds to claim ignorance. And therefore, to reject Him brings greater condemnation. Ever since the Fall, the world has been sinning against Light, but never had the world sinned against so *much* Light! The world is robbed of its excuses when it confronts Christ.

The better the world becomes acquainted with Christ, the more difficult it is for it to receive Him. And what is true of the Master is true of His followers.

Are we prepared for such hatred? Or are we more concerned about what the world thinks of us than we are of what God thinks of us? The serious follower of Christ will have to choose between fear of man and the fear of the Lord. It is not possible to have both!

■ The Persecution of the World

Christ says, "Remember the word that I said to you, 'A slave is not greater than his master.' If they persecuted Me, they will also persecute you; if they kept My word, they will keep yours also" (v. 20). Christ was persecuted— the Herodians, Sadducees, and Pharisees sought Him as a hawk seeks its prey. His followers cannot expect better treatment.

In fact, Christ taught that those who would persecute His followers will actually think they are doing God a favor! "They will make you outcasts from the synagogues; but an hour is coming for everyone who kills you to think he is offering service to God" (16:2). This, of course, was fulfilled in the days of the early church, when the Jews believed they were on God's side though they put Christ to death and persecuted the disciples. Most of the early apostles died violent deaths—Paul was murdered by Nero; Peter, according to tradition, was crucified upside down; and James was beheaded. All that done by leaders who claimed to be doing God a favor.

Though Christ's words have immediate application to the disciples, persecution has happened throughout church history. During the Inquisition, the teaching of the church was assumed to be correct and often true followers of Jesus were put to death. All kinds of atrocities have been justified in the name of Christ.

Today, there is a myth that the world is more tolerant than it used to be in accepting "both points of view." We pride ourselves in pluralism; the teaching that all different kinds of political and spiritual views can be held in a society such as the United States. It's easy to be deceived into thinking that the world is less antagonistic than it used to be. But the rise of contemporary secular humanism has proven this to be false. By stressing the rigid separation of church and state, there are many in our society who would take away our freedoms. Some are lobbying for laws that would make it illegal to meet for prayer on a university campus; others want religion totally expunged from all areas of political and moral life. When humanism is in the minority, it pleads for tolerance and pluralism; but when it is in control, it attempts to stamp out all religion, particularly Christianity.

In America, Christians pride themselves in being "law-abiding citizens." That is a compliment only in a country whose laws reflect biblical values. But as our culture moves from its Christians foundation, it will soon become necessary for us to be lawbreakers. Christians have always been compelled to break laws. Whether it be Tyndale, who translated the Bible into English, or Bunyan, who was jailed for preaching the Gospel, these and thousands like them found it necessary to break laws. Like the early apostles, they said, "Whether it is right in the sight of God to give heed to you rather than to God, you be the judge; for we cannot stop speaking what we have seen and heard" (Acts 4:19-20).

Since humanism and Christianity have coexisted in America for 200 years, many expect that they will continue to do so. But as humanism becomes stronger, it will become more intolerant. Hitler, Stalin, and China's Mao are good examples of secularism brought to its ultimate conclusion. When the state becomes a substitute for God, this false god will attack the true and the living God.

As of now, we need not fear physical persecution in the United States. But the true Christian will attract the disdain, hatred, and contempt of the world in other ways. You may be ostracized from your peer group, denied a promotion, or ridiculed for being a relic from previous generations. You will personally be disliked if you live with meticulous integrity and separation from worldly values. Although we may be exempt from torture and death, the basic contempt of mankind for Christ comes to the surface in every culture where the church shines brightly in the world. "And indeed, all who desire to live godly in Christ Jesus will be persecuted" (2 Tim. 3:12).

Christ says, "A slave is not greater than his master." If we think we have the right to live without persecution, we are lacking humility—we are actually placing ourselves above Christ. Should we escape the antagonism that He incurred because we are greater than He? I think not. The brighter our lamp burns, the more the world is repelled.

Back in 1971, a revival came to many churches in Western Canada. It made news in the secular press because of the number of people going to stores and other businesses to make restitution for past wrongdoing. Whether it was paying unpaid income tax, or admitting dishonesty in business dealings, or going to the Canadian border to confess they had lied about goods brought over from the United States—hundreds of people were willing to do anything to be fully right with God and man. When these Christians displayed such a desire for righteousness, the world both admired and hated them. On the one hand, the people of the world were thankful that the Christians had the courage to make past wrongs right; but on the other hand, they deeply resented such integrity. For in the process of seeing righteousness at work in the lives of others, they saw their own hidden sins.

■ The Misunderstanding of the World

Why would the world hate Christ? Jesus said, "But all these things they will do to you for My name's sake, because they do not know the One who sent Me" (15:21). The world is ignorant of God; that's why they hate Christ. If they had known God the Father, they would have recognized Jesus Christ as His Son. As Carson says, "If people knew the Father *before* Jesus came in history, then they would recognize Jesus upon His arrival. Failure to know Jesus, therefore, testifies to ignorance of God before

Jesus' arrival."[3] Now that Christ has come, we can say with equal authority that if a person does not know Christ, he does not know God the Father.

Deism, which had a profound effect in early American history, held that God could be known apart from Christ. The Deist said that through nature, we can come to know God. Judaism also claimed to have a correct knowledge of God, but Christ strongly contradicted such notions. "He who hates Me hates My Father also" (v. 23). Theologically, it is impossible to drive a wedge between God the Father and God the Son. To honor the Son is to honor the Father; to dishonor the Son is to dishonor the Father.

When hard pressed, the world cannot really explain why it hates Christ. "They hated Me without a cause," Christ says (v. 25). Why would anyone hate Christ, who went about doing good? Think of the number of people He healed, the sermons He preached, and the good work His disciples were trained to do. Yet, they hated Him, not because He was evil, but because He was good and showed them up for who they really were.

The Jews claimed that they wanted Christ crucified for theological reasons because He made Himself the Son of God. But Pilate, who was a careful student of human nature and who knew much more about Christ than he let on, understood the real motive: "For he was aware that the chief priests had delivered Him up because of envy" (Mark 15:10). So that's why Jesus was crucified! He was too popular, too successful, too pure.

Yes, they hated Christ without a cause, but even this fell within the circle of God's providence. For Christ said, "But they had done this in order that the Word may be fulfilled that is written in their Law, 'They hated Me without a cause' " (v. 25). Christ makes an apparent reference to Psalm 69:4. The hatred of the world is to be expected, and fits into God's larger plan.

These disciples would soon be traveling in the Roman world that believed political unity could be maintained only by loyalty to Caesar. Once a year, every citizen was required to burn a pinch of incense to Caesar and to confess "Caesar is lord." As long as he worshiped the Emperor, he could worship any other god he wanted. But the Christians throughout the Empire couldn't do that, and they paid for it with their lives. Today, we still have the same challenge, though it may not appear as dramatic. Even today we must yet choose between Caesar and Christ.

■ Some Important Lessons

Let's summarize Christ's teaching about the world. First, His followers and the world are *irreconcilable*. There is no common ground between them. There must be antagonism and strife. The world stands in opposition to everything that Christ holds dear. As one writer put it, "However it may be covered over, there is a gulf, as in some . . . American canyons; the towering banks may be very near—only a yard or two seem to separate them; but they go down for thousands and thousands of feet, and never get any nearer each other, and between them at the bottom a black, sullen river flows."[4]

As already emphasized, let's not be deceived into thinking that the world is getting more and more tolerant. It definitely is not. As worldly values gain in power, the world will attempt to crush the teachings of Christ and His followers.

Second, believers cannot be friends with both Christ and the world. As James put it, "You adulteresses, do you not know that friendship with the world is hostility toward God? Therefore, whoever wishes to be a friend of the world makes himself an enemy of God" (4:4). You can have the friendship of Christ or the friendship of the world, but you cannot have both at the same time! The kingdom of the world which is passing away, and the kingdom of Christ are heading in two different directions, led by two sovereigns who are antagonistic to each other. You cannot serve both, nor can you benefit from both at the same time.

Third, if we have not felt the antagonism of unbelievers who touch our lives, isn't it likely because we are lacking in our Christian commitment? A Christian who is popular with the world is a contradiction in terms. If we have not attracted the scorn of the world, it may well be because we have muddled our Christian witness. As F.B. Meyer says, in the dim twilight, one is easily able to mistake friend and foe!

Joy comes in being persecuted for the cause of Christ. "Blessed are you when men cast insults at you, and persecute you, and say all kinds of evil against you falsely, on account of Me. Rejoice, and be glad, for your reward in heaven is great, for so they persecuted the prophets who were before you" (Matt. 5:11-12).

One of the reasons that the early church was so invincible was the exhilaration of joy they experienced in persecution. They were thrilled to think that they were counted worthy to suffer shame for the name of Christ. Little wonder that the church and the world were two distinct entities in those days. There was night, and then there was day—there was no twilight in which friend or foe could be mistaken.

Someone has written that to be hated is uncomfortable, but it is "infinitely more damning to be blandly ignored and overlooked, contemptuously dismissed as a set of children playing their futile childish games—doing no good, of course, but not much harm, and so left to amuse themselves with their innocuous pastimes."

In America, we are often blandly ignored. We arouse no opposition because the brand of Christianity we have adopted does not stand in opposition to the worldly values that swirl around us. We must confess that we have not caused the world to see itself for what it is. As lightning is attracted to those objects which best conduct electricity, so the hatred of the world is aroused by Christians who are attuned with God.

The world has an ample supply of hatred stored up that will be unleashed at any time we seek to be true followers of Christ. In back of it is the power of Satan, who hates Christ and does everything he can to trip up His followers. But as Paul says, we shall only reign with Him if we suffer with Him!

This section in the Upper Room discourse effectively puts an end to the widespread belief that success and wealth are the inevitable results of living a committed Christian life. The gospel of prosperity deceives people who cannot distinguish between pursuing God and pursuing their own personal happiness. Christ promised that in the world we will have tribulation.

Can you think of any instances of ridicule you experienced because of your witness for Christ? If you are still not convinced that the world is antagonistic to Christ, here is a challenge: boldly apply Christian principles in the marketplace coupled with a loving witness for Christ. Some will respect you; others will pity you; others will resent you.

Bravery for Christ is the only indisputable proof of our love for Him. It comes to a matter of simplicity: Do we love Him more than the opinions of men?

A servant is not above His master.

NOTES

1. Maclaren, *With Christ,* p. 225.
2. Meyer, *Expositions,* p. 135.
3. Carson, D.A., *The Farewell Discourse and Final Prayer of Jesus* (Grand Rapids: Baker Book House, 1980), p. 225.
4. Maclaren, *With Christ,* p. 225.

CHAPTER 8

CULTIVATING A
WITNESSING
HEART

JOHN 16:5-15

This little jingle can be easily proven true:

> Convince a man against his will,
> He'll be of the same opinion still.

Have you ever tried to change someone's opinion, especially about religion? You'll soon find that prejudice, narrow-mindness and sheer stubbornness will surface. And it doesn't matter whether you are Catholic, Protestant, or Jewish!

Consider a young eighteen-year-old boy who accepted Christ as his Saviour. All of his guilt is gone; peace comes to his heart. He can hardly wait to share the Good News. When he arrives home, he tells his parents that they also can become Christians by repenting of sin and by faith, receiving the gift of life from Christ. He's surprised when they do not share his enthusiasm. "You're off your rocker; your elevator doesn't go all the way to the top! Just get over this nonsense because we are Christians already."

He can't believe it! It's like finding gold and telling others where they can find some too, and yet being greeted with a cold stare. Instead of coming to Christ, the boy's parents tenaciously hang on to their religious beliefs, such as they are. They don't see themselves as sinners needing a personal Saviour.

This young convert must understand a basic truth: *no man comes to Christ without the power of the Spirit drawing him.* Nothing is as inflexible as the human will. Unless God does a great work in the life of a person, no one would ever receive the gift of salvation through Jesus Christ.

When Jesus was preparing the disciples for His departure, He said the Comforter would take His place. There would be no significant loss as far as the disciples and their followers were concerned. In fact, it was to their advantage that He would go away so that the Comforter would come. As Maclaren puts it, "He is nearer us when He leaves us, and works with us and in us more mightily from the throne than He did upon the earth."[1] Then speaking of the supposed advantage the disciples had to be personally with Christ, Maclaren continues, "We have lost nothing that they had which was worth the keeping; and we have gained a great deal which they had not."[2] Believers are indwelt, empowered, and strengthened by the presence of the Holy Spirit in the world.

The Holy Spirit, however, will have quite a different mission to the world. Jesus said that the Spirit cannot be received by the world, but the Holy Spirit will have the responsibility of drawing the unconverted to Christ. Though the disciples felt helpless in the face of the world, Christ dispelled the gloom by giving the assurance that the Holy Spirit would confront the world directly: "And He, when He comes, will convict the world concerning sin, and righteousness, and judgment" (John 16:8).

What does that word *convict* mean? Does it mean that the Holy Spirit will prove the world guilty? No, the world is already guilty before God. "He that believeth on the Son hath everlasting life, but he that believeth not the Son shall not see life, but the wrath of God abideth on him" (John 3:36, kjv). But the Spirit will awaken the world's consciousness of guilt, and people will be brought to the point of personal faith. In effect, the Holy Spirit takes on the role of a prosecutor; He enables men and women to see themselves in God's courtroom and recognize their need of His mercy before it is too late.

Of what will the Holy Spirit convince the world? Christ specifies three distinct areas of truth.

■ The One Sin: Unbelief

The Holy Spirit will convince the world "concerning sin, because they do not believe in Me" (v. 9). That is, the Spirit will convince people of the *reality* of sin. Many people don't believe they are sinners because they define sin externally. Usually, they compare themselves with someone who is worse than they are! But God judges us by what we think, by what we are deep inside. Not one of us would like to expose our thoughts to others. If we could see the hatred, doubt, blasphemy, and lust in the human heart, we would all be disillusioned. Christ taught that evil comes from within the human heart and eventually is acted out in experience. But it's those inward thoughts that God judges, whether we act them out or not.

The expression "concerning sin, because they do not believe in Me" reminds us that the epitome of sin is unbelief. The greatest sin that a man can commit is not murder or adultery, but rejecting Jesus Christ. "The one who does not believe God has made Him a liar" (1 John 5:10). The unbeliever makes God a liar, and insults His only begotten Son.

While on earth, Christ did many miracles, but the Pharisees attributed His awesome power to Satan. Christ said that their sin would not be forgiven, either in this world or in the world to come. This unpardonable sin, in a word, is *unbelief*. The same sin can be committed today by people who have hardened their hearts against God and refused to submit themselves to His authority.

Conviction of sin is a sure sign of the Spirit's ministry. Although not everyone who receives Christ must be overwhelmed with guilt (children can often believe without such a strong sense of sin), yet each in his own way must understand his deep need. The old adage is still true: we must get people lost before we can get them saved!

■ The One Standard: Righteousness

Christ further defines the work of the Spirit as bringing conviction "concerning righteousness, because I go to the Father, and you no longer behold Me" (v. 10). Perhaps the best way to translate this is to say that the Holy Spirit will convince the world of its need for God's righteousness—by making the world realize the poverty of its own righteousness.

There are two kinds of righteousness—God's and man's. "For all of us have become like one who is unclean, and all our righteous deeds are like a filthy garment" (Isa. 64:6). The Apostle Paul spoke of the Israelites: "For not knowing about God's righteousness, and seeking to establish their own, they did not subject themselves to the righteousness of God" (Rom. 10:3). Human righteousness falls short of what God requires. It's not only that God has more righteousness than we do; He has a different kind of righteousness. And God only accepts His own! That's why we need to have the righteousness of Christ credited to our account.

In a restaurant, I asked a woman what she would say if God were to ask, "Why should I let you into heaven?" She replied, "My husband and run an honest business, and I earned more than $1,200 for our church in a bake sale." Very gently, I assured her that human righteousness has never been accepted by God and never will be. All of the human goodness that has ever been done on the earth since the time of Adam and Eve, all added together, will never change God's mind regarding a single sinner!

The woman looked surprised, but still thought that her righteousness would contribute somewhat to her salvation. Only the Holy Spirit can convince her that she needs a different kind of righteousness. Christ adds, "Because I go to the Father and you no longer behold Me." When He was on earth, He was convicting the world of sin, but now the Holy Spirit would take over that responsibility. Earlier, He said that the Holy Spirit would "bear witness" regarding Him (John 15:26). Through the work of the Spirit, men and women come to see their need for the gift of righteousness.

Aren't you glad that our sin was credited toward Christ so that His righteousness could be given to us? In the words of the hymn writer:

> Jesus, Thy blood and righteousness
> My beauty art, my glorious dress.

■ The One Danger: Judgment

The work of the Holy spirit is not yet finished. He will also convict "concerning judgment, because the ruler of this world has been judged" (v. 11). Once again, the Holy Spirit will convince the world of its false judgments and will help them understand the true judgment of God. The world has always been wrong in its fundamental assessment of spiritual things. Think of how badly it has interpreted the facts: at the cross, the world thought that Jesus Christ's ministry had ended, but actually, it was there that Satan was decisively defeated. The world considered Christ to be a blasphemer, but didn't realize that it was the spotless Son of God they were crucifying. The Holy Spirit will point out these wrong evaluations "because the ruler of this world has been judged" (v. 11). So the Holy Spirit will point to the cross as the defeat of Satan and the victory of Christ.

Of course, the Holy Spirit will also remind the world of the judgment of God. Paul says that a day is coming when God will judge the secrets of men through Christ (Rom. 2:16). At the trial the prosecutor will bring all of the facts into the courtroom for examination. Actually, *the whole world is out on bail, and God is waiting to round up its inhabitants and bring them into the courtroom.* Fortunately, those who have believed on Jesus Christ are exempt from God's judgment. They may lose rewards in heaven, but they will not stand where the judgment of God has already fallen.

However much men and women may protest against belief in God, they innately believe in a day of reckoning. If there was no coming judgment, all of the wrongs of the world would never be rectified, and justice could never be served. Stalin and Hitler would go unpunished and the universe would remain fundamentally unjust. Something within all of us says there is an appointment with the final judge. No one will be able to post bond, escape across the border, or plead insanity. All of the facts will be brought out with clarity in the presence of the searchlight of God's holiness. Someone has said that the day of Judgment will be so bad that, for some, hell will be a welcome refuge from the presence of the Almighty. The Spirit convicts the world of the judgment that took place on the cross but also the impending judgment of the wicked.

What a welcome these words must have received in the minds of the disciples! That hostile environment called the world was not formidable. The Spirit would bear witness and convince men and women of the truth of Christ. As Barclay says, "When you think of it, it is an amazing thing that men should put their trust for all eternity in a crucified Jewish criminal."[3] This can be brought about only by the work of the Holy Spirit.

Can the work of the Spirit be resisted? Yes. Stephen, when addressing his enemies, said, "You men who are stiff-necked and uncircumcised in heart and ears are always resisting the Holy Spirit; you are doing just as your fathers did" (Acts 7:51). However, theologians such as Augustine and Calvin believed that there is an irresistible work of the Holy Spirit that draws the elect to Christ. Our Lord has said, "All that the Father gives Me shall come to Me" (John 6:37). However, let's not interpret that word *irresistible* to mean that God overrides the human will. Rather, it means that God works through the human will to bring individuals to saving faith. This is sometimes spoken of as the "effectual call": "And whom He predestinated, He also called; and whom He called, these He also justified; and whom He justified, these He also glorified" (Rom. 8:30).

Regardless of our understanding of the doctrine of election, it is undeniable that no man can come to Christ on his own. As Christ stated repeatedly, "No one can come to Me, unless it has been granted him from the Father" (John 6:65).

■ The One Channel: Believers

What means does the Holy Spirit use to convince the world of its need of Christ? Christ says, "And you will bear witness also, because you have been with Me from the beginning" (15:27). Unmistakably, Christ says that the Spirit will work *through us*.

Seldom does God work in a vacuum. He does not often convict a person of sin as he/she walks down the street. If God does that, it's usually because the person has already been confronted with the truth. God expects us to be active in our witness; we must be the ones to share the Good News so that the Holy Spirit can make the truth come alive to those who have heard. We do not have to argue or to prove the truth (though presenting evidence may be at times appropriate); rather, we simply have to "bear witness." The Spirit is to do the work.

During the summer of 1984, my wife, our children, and I visited China. When that country was closed to the Gospel after the revolution of 1949, all mission agencies agreed that there were approximately one half million believers in the country. The Communist government instituted programs of harassment, persecution, and death for those who were found to be Christians. During the cultural revolution, which took place in the '60s, many others were put into concentration camps, Bibles were burned, and all churches were closed. Many observers thought the church in China had died, that Communism had done what was generally believed to be impossible: namely, to exterminate the church.

Such predictions overlooked God's power. Now that the country has opened up, we have discovered that perhaps 25 million believers live in that great land. But how did they hear the Gospel message? There is no Christian television, no Christian radio, and it's against the law to hand out Christian literature or even personally witness. Yet the church grew remarkably in the midst of repression and strong political opposition. The answer is that believers began to realize that the Word of Christ could only reach others *through them.* So believers would witness quietly, without fanfare. Often, they would take risks not knowing whether the person to whom they spoke was a friend or a foe. But slowly, sometimes imperceptibly, the church began to grow. Actually, whether they realized it or not, the believers were duplicating what we read in Acts 8: "Therefore, those who had been scattered went about preaching the Word" (v. 4). Satan tried to blow the fire out through persecution, but in the process he blew it all over the landscape!

How does the Holy Spirit do His finest work? Through the lives of other believers. That's why there are so many exhortations in the Bible for Christians to pray for one another, and so few that say we should pray for the unsaved world. The obvious implication is that if Christians are what they should be, the world will be confronted with Christ through them and the convicting power of the Spirit will draw men and women to the Saviour. God's best method is still to work through devoted and holy men and women.

What is more important in witnessing—a man's life or his words? That's like asking which wing of an airplane is most important—the right or the left. Both are necessary. If we speak without living the life, we will bring reproach on Christ's name. If we only live an exemplary life, but do not give an explanation for our lifestyle, we only draw attention to ourselves. Like the person who lamented his breakdown in communication by saying, "I pointed to the moon, but all you saw was my finger." We must get beyond ourselves to pointing out Christ.

Many people today are restless, angry, and dissatisfied, not knowing that the Holy Spirit is trying to reach them. They may go to a psychiatrist, take tranquilizers, and do all they can to quiet their uneasy feeling within. It's been said that there are people whom psychiatrists are trying to make comfortable whom God is trying to make uncomfortable! They don't recognize their discomfort as the voice of God.

Some time ago, I read about a miser who stored all of his money in the cellar of his cottage, and from time to time would take it out and count it (apparently he liked the feel of it). Two thieves watched him through the window one evening as he counted his money and finally put it in a safe place beneath the floor. Then the man took a drink and laid down to sleep. A few hours later, his dog began to bark violently. The man became angry with the dog and told him to be quiet. Once again the dog barked, and the man cursed him and told him to shut up. When the dog continued barking, the man became so irritated that he took a gun and shot the animal. Then while he slept, the thieves broke in and stole his money.

To the person reading this who has never accepted Christ, let me give you a word of warning: *don't stifle the one voice that can save you.* Remember the Holy Spirit has been sent to the world to convince the world of sin. If you do not respond openly to His promptings, you will be damned. Without His gracious work, no one can be saved. Don't stifle the promptings of the Spirit through alcoholism, drugs, pleasure, and selfish pursuits. Only Christ can save you and only the Spirit can draw you to Him.

NOTES

1. Maclaren, *With Christ,* p. 271.
2. Ibid.

CHAPTER 9

SEEKING A DISCERNING HEART

JOHN 16:16-33

Somewhere I read a story about a boy reading a novel in the living room. His mother called to him, "Come help me in the kitchen." But he responded, "No, Mom . . . right now the villain has the hero down and is about to kill him, so I have to see how the story ends." His mother persisted, "I said you are to come right now to help with the dishes." Knowing that he had to go, he flipped to the last page of the book and read it. There he discovered that the hero didn't die after all; the villain was killed, and the hero won. When the boy walked into the kitchen, he said, "That villain is doing OK in chapter five, but is he ever in for a surprise when he gets to the last page!"

One of the marks of spiritual maturity is the ability to judge matters by long-term consequences rather than immediate rewards. It's easy to misinterpret who is ahead and who is losing without a long-range perspective.

What appears to be success could be failure in disguise. What we call "good" sometimes turns out to be a curse.

One fundamental rule of interpretation is that we should base our conclusions on long-range consequences and not short-term pleasures. Freud is quoted as saying that the mark of maturity is to be able to postpone pleasures. That's sound advice, regardless of whether you respect the source.

Let's take sexual sin as an example. The person who tastes fleeting sexual pleasure is tempted to do it again and again. And as one writer has pointed out, discipline becomes so difficult because we then fight against a whole series of immediate rewards that are in competition with immediate frustrations and later rewards. The mature Christian is willing to postpone immediate pleasures for long-term ones.

It's been said that people today know the price of everything but the value of nothing. Knowing what to laugh about and what to cry about is not as easy as it seems. Some people who are having a great time would be sorrowful if they knew what lay ahead. If only they took eternity into account, they would soon find out that their judgments were superficial.

Discernment is the key word. The ability to distinguish the permanent from the temporary, the seen from the unseen, belongs to the spiritually mature.

Christ contrasted the opinion of the unbelieving, unregenerate world with that of His disciples. What He taught is that the world would rejoice in His impending death; the disciples would be sorrowful. But in the end, the tables would be reversed: the disciples would rejoice and the world would be condemned. If we want to have a whole heart in a confused world, we'd better have God's long-range perspective. His interpretation of events gives us the reassurance that obedience to His will has long-term results.

■ The World's Joy Is Short-lived

Christ predicted that the world would rejoice at His death: "Truly, truly, I say to you, that you will weep and lament, but the world will rejoice; you will be sorrowful, but your sorrow will be turned into joy" (John 16:20).

Once that Christ was on the cross, official religion was relieved of a man who not only was regarded as a nuisance, but also a threat to the prideful religiosity of the day. However much the religious leaders may have pretended to grieve over the crucifixion of a human being, make no mistake: Christ's death to them was as welcome as a doctor's pronouncement that a cancerous growth had just disappeared.

They hated Christ because He exposed their ignorance. He asked embarrassing questions such as, "The baptism of John, was it from heaven or of man?" If they answered, "From heaven," they knew that Christ's follow-up question would be, "Then why didn't you believe him?" If they answered, "From men," they would be in trouble with the people who regarded John as a prophet. Either way, they would lose. So they opted for silence.

Remember when Christ asked, "What do you think about the Christ, whose Son is He?" They answered, "The son of David." Christ replied, "Then how does David in the Spirit call Him Lord, saying, 'The Lord said unto My Lord, "Sit at My right hand until I put Thine enemies beneath Thy feet" ' "? (Matt. 22:44)

They should have known the answer to this puzzle: In Psalm 101, the Lord Jehovah speaks to the Lord *Adoni* asking Him to sit at His right hand. God the Father is talking to God the Son. Yet, although the Son is eternal, He is still the son of David because Christ was born as a man through the Davidic line. What Christ wanted the Pharisees to admit is that the Messiah is God. But they had not thought through their convictions. Nor did they want to admit to the deity of Christ. So again they said nothing.

Christ exposed their ignorance, but even more humiliating, He exposed their sin. He called them "whitewashed sepulchers" who were clean without but foul within. He spoke of murder, adultery, and covetousness as sins of the heart. He told them that they were scrupulous about things that didn't matter. But they were tolerant of sins that they enjoyed.

Understandably, when Christ was on the cross, they said, "Good riddance!" Now they could go back to their own comfort zone—attracting attention with their piety without surrendering anything that was truly costly.

So the world rejoiced. But it was too soon for a party.

They saw Christ's death as good news, but they were blinded to the bad news. Yes, Christ was dead; but not for long. And in the end, they will have to meet Him one more time when He returns as judge.

The world looks at life through the wrong end of a telescope. People who are laughing should be crying. Like a criminal who rejoices that he is above the crowd, but doesn't know that he is actually on the gallows . . . so unbelievers of the world think they can ignore God. They don't know their doom is just around the corner. The verdict of the future reverses the verdict of the moment.

In the Book of Revelation, there is a story of the devil's Christmas. Two of God's witnesses (possibly Moses and Elijah) have just been killed and their bodies laid out on the streets. At last, the world has snuffed out the lives of those who were spoiling their fun. It's party time: "And those who dwell on the earth will rejoice over them and make merry; and they will send gifts to one another, because these two prophets tormented those that dwell on the earth" (Rev. 11:10).

But three and a half days later, God gives their bodies life and they stand on their feet. Then we read: "And in that hour, there was a great earthquake and a tenth of the city fell; and 7,000 people were killed in the earthquake and the rest were terrified and gave glory to the God of heaven" (11:13).

The party is over.

Christ told the disciples not to be deceived by the interpretations of the world. The world would rejoice over His death, but this one scene was not the whole act. Tomorrow the curtain would rise again.

In other words, many people will be shocked when they get to the last page!

■ Believers Have Short-lived Sorrow

As for the disciples, Jesus predicted that they would "weep and lament." Christ did not chide them for the sorrow they would show. There is nothing particularly spiritual about taking the hurts of life with emotionless stoicism. Jesus was their closest and best friend. Their relationship with Him had been forged on the anvil of sorrow and the rejection of the world. You may forget those with whom you have laughed, but you will never forget those with whom you have cried.

The disciples would be like sheep without a shepherd; orphans bereft of their best friend. The One whom they had trusted at great personal cost would be dead. They believed that the earthly kingdom predicted by the Old Testament prophets would be established immediately. None of the disciples understood clearly that Christ's death and resurrection plus 2,000 years of church history would precede the kingdom era. So when Christ died, the disciples faced an uncertain future. Their hopes died with Him.

The two who walked on their way to Emmaus after Christ's death were living through an emotional earthquake. They said to the stranger, "But we were hoping that it was He who was going to redeem Israel. Indeed, beside all this, it is the third day since these things happened" (Luke 24:21). They saw their hero insulted and forsaken. What is worse, they now believed that they had been misled. Their sorrow was intense, and there was no reason for them to think that it would vanish.

But Christ's followers would learn that they had not been led astray. In the end, Christ was as trustworthy as He seemed to be. *Their temporary sorrow would be turned into permanent joy.* It's not just that joy would follow their sorrow; the event that caused them sorrow would give them joy. Christ adds, "Whenever a woman is in travail she has sorrow because her hour has come; but when she gives birth to the child, she remembers the anguish no more, for joy that has been born into the world" (John 16: 21).

This pregnant woman is a picture of the church throughout its 2,000-year history. When you read the history of the church, you find it is a story of pain and grief. There has been persecution, plus doctrinal and moral deviations. There have been times when paganism crept into the church and when the issues of the Gospel were blurred. Even redeemed humanity has the imperfections of our fallen nature. The sorrow of the church will continue, but eventually turn into blessings and joy.

Perhaps the best way for us to explain God's ability to take evil and turn it into a blessing is to look at the cross. Let me ask: Was the death of Christ evil or was it good? In one sense, it was the greatest crime that was ever committed. Wicked hands crucified the sinless Son of God without any reason except that He revealed the evil in their own hearts. Yet, Paul said, "But may it never be that I should boast, except in the cross of our Lord Jesus Christ, through which the world has been crucified to me, and I to the world" (Gal. 6:14). From this great evil, the blessing of the Lord came. To quote Alexander Maclaren, "The same death which, before the Resurrection, drew a pall of darkness over the heavens and draped the earth in mourning, by reason of that Resurrection which swept away the cloud and brought out the sunshine, became the source of joy. A dead Christ was the church's despair; a dead and risen Christ is the church's triumph."[1]

Perhaps God will eventually treat all evil as He did the cross—He will use it for a greater good. That which caused us the greatest grief on earth may give us the greatest joy in heaven. As Paul said, "For momentary, light affliction is producing for us an eternal weight of glory far beyond all comprehension, while we look not at the things which are seen, but at the things which are not seen; for the things which are seen are temporal, but the things which are not seen are eternal" (2 Cor. 4:17-18). If we could have a measuring tape that would go from the earth to the farthest star, our years on earth would be but the width of a pencil line. In comparison, the rest of the measuring tape would extend billions of light years into the universe.

Our sorrows will be turned into gladness; the gladness of the world will lead to permanent distress. The world can never dispose of Christ. Though they may consistently ignore Him, eventually every human being will have to contend with Him.

While one earth, Christ was summoned before Pilate, but in that day Pilate will be brought before Christ:

For after all, it is only just for God to repay with

affliction those who afflict you, and to give relief to you who are afflicted, and to us as well when the Lord Jesus shall be revealed from heaven with His mighty angels in flaming fire, dealing out retribution to those who do not know God and to those who do not obey the Gospel of our Lord Jesus. And these will pay the penalty of eternal destruction, away from the presence of the Lord and from the glory of His power, when He comes to be glorified in His saints on that day, and to be marveled at among all who have believed—for our testimony to you was believed (2 Thes. 1:6-10).

■ Help for Our Sorrows

The disciples did not understand that Christ would return to them after His death and resurrection. But our Lord wanted them to be aware that a day is coming when they would be able to pray effectively to the Father. He also promised them renewed understanding: "And in that day you will ask Me no question. Truly, truly, I say to you, if you shall ask the Father for anything, He will give it to you in My name" (John 16:23). The kind of questions they have been asking will become unnecessary. The illumination of the Holy Spirit along with fellowship with the risen Christ will clarify the nature of Christ's mission. In that day, they will ask in His name, and they will receive that their joy may be made full.

When Christ says, "These things I have spoken to you in figurative language," He is referring to veiled speech in contrast to the plain speaking that He will have with them after His resurrection. In that day, they will know that the Father also loves them and that they can pray to Him directly in Christ's name. Until now, the disciples could not have asked anything in the name of Christ because His mediatorial work is dependent upon the Cross.

Christ makes a close association between joy and their new privilege of prayer. D.A. Carson says, "If obedience to Christ makes us warm with joy, and if fruitful petitionary prayer to our loving God and Father completes our joy, then we are approximating Jesus' expectation of what His followers should experience this side of the cross."[2]

As we near the end of John 16, the disciples say that they finally understand what Christ has been trying to teach them. "Lo, now You are speaking plainly and are not using a figure of speech. Now we know that You know all things, and have no need for anyone to question You; by this we believe that You came from God" (16:29-30). Christ is pleased, but not so sure that they understand sufficiently to overcome the hurdle of the Crucifixion which lay ahead. He tells them that they will scatter from Him when the crunch comes; they do not fully understand this, for they have not yet received the fullness of the Holy Spirit, who will later give them both revelation and strength. Christ lets the disciples know that they will fail Him so that when it happens they will know that it did not take Him by surprise. He reminds them that they will have further persecution in this world, but they could be of good cheer, for He had overcome the world.

Here then, is the final example of the two opposing perspectives. For the moment, the world seems to be better off than the disciples, but all of that will change. The world has the advantage of *clinging* to values that are comfortable, predictable, and lead to fulfillment. For a time, the world can go on without the painful experience of having its sin exposed. From its pedestal of self-congratulatory knowledge, it can ridicule the followers of a Man who made a nuisance of Himself by asking probing questions and doing miracles. Seen through one set of glasses, it appears as if the people of the world have taken the safe and most pleasant route.

But there will be a great reversal: their joy will be turned into sorrow. They will be encountering storms that will terrify and eventually end in an excruciating day of judgment. In contrast, the disciples are to be pitied for the moment. They have chosen the lonely path fraught with unexpected peril, but God is with them. They can over-come the world because Christ has.

If we want to be committed followers of Christ, part of the price we will pay is faith that His perspective is more accurate than that of the world. We will have to continue to believe even in the midst of sadness and the confusion of conflicting purposes. God's will may often appear to be dark; the path of holiness may lead to gloom. But in the end, Christ has promised us joy.

Some time ago, I read a story about a missionary couple who returned from a foreign country on board a ship. Journeying with them was a tour group of celebrities who partied the whole route, drinking, and living in sensuality. When the ship arrived at the harbor, a delegation met this distinguished group, but no one was there to greet the missionaries, who had given five years of their lives to serve the King of kings.

One day the missionary poured out his heart to God about the matter. He rehearsed the facts: the people of the world were treated with more appreciation than he and his wife. After his talk with the Lord, he returned to his wife radiant with joy. The burden had lifted.

What made the difference? He explained how he had told the Lord that the people of the world were welcomed home, whereas he and his wife had not been welcomed home. But then, he said, "It was as if the Lord said, 'Wait a moment; you're not home yet!'"

When we look at life from God's perspective we will

discern the difference between what lasts and what doesn't. We will stick with Christ regardless of how dark our world becomes. In the end, our deepest sorrows will become our greatest joys.

The discerning heart knows that the last page has yet to be written.

NOTES

1. Maclaren, *With Christ*, p. 318.
2. Carson, *The Farewell Discourse*, p. 165.

CHAPTER 10

FINDING A FULFILLED HEART

JOHN 17:1-5

A man with AIDS got in touch with me recently to get some perspective on how to spend the last few years of his life. Here is what he said word for word: "I need some counsel because I do not want to waste my final years as I have the rest. I am at peace with myself, but want to live my last days for the glory of God."

Samuel Johnson observed that nothing focuses the mind like knowing that one is to be hanged. To think about peripheral issues becomes impossible. Trivial matters separate from ultimate ones with unusual speed and clarity. What would you do if you knew you would die tomorrow? Many of us would not be able to respond like John Wesley, who said that he would not change his schedule if he received such news. For some of us, death will catch us with unfinished business. Too late, we may discover that we lived with wrong priorities. We may have been climbing the ladder of success, but to our shame will discover that our ladder was leaning against the wrong wall.

Of course, it need not be that way. In John 17, Christ pulls the curtain back to give us some intimate glimpses into His own thoughts and feelings on the evening before His crucifixion. We almost feel guilty reading this prayer because of the intimacy expressed between the Father and the Son. But Christ intended that we should listen so we can better understand why He died a fulfilled man. Here are the inner thoughts of One who had a whole heart in a broken world. When under pressure, His motives, aspirations, and intentions all come to the surface.

Christ understood full well the horror that He would experience the next day. Ahead of Him lay Gethsemane, with its intolerable emotional turbulence. He would spend the night in solitary confinement and in the morning be abused, publicly humiliated, and crucified. When he would bear the sin of the world, there would be the cry of anguish, "My God, My God, why hast Thou forsaken Me?"

Yet, remarkably, this prayer mentions nothing about these unspeakable horrors. He does not plead that the pain be lessened; He does not ask that the agony be condensed so that He can get it over with quickly. In the hours before painful suffering, his concern is for the honor of the Father and the success of His disciples. Here is the final earthly legacy of Christ. Here, for all to see, is the example of One who knew what it was to live untainted by the selfish motives of fallen humanity.

Please don't make the mistake of thinking that the principles by which Christ lived don't apply to you. His single-minded determination to do the Father's will is an example that can be yours and mine. Yes, there is a chasm between us and Christ, but there are many similarities between us as well. Our lives are also planned by God the Father; we too will have to experience the humiliation of death. And our motivation for living should be the same as His. Here we see the full meaning of the expression "to be in the world but not of the world."

If you are serious about living a godly life in an ungodly world, this is a prayer that should be studied and memorized. Christ shows the motivation of His own heart, but also prays for His disciples and for all those who will eventually believe on Him. As we shall see in another chapter, all of us are included in His prayer. We need the strength and protection that His intercession provides.

The prayer has three sections in John 17. In verses 1 through 5, Christ prays for Himself; in verses 6 through 19, He prays for the disciples; and in verses 20 through 26, He prays for the entire church. The last two verses summarize His special relationship with His people and provide a summary of His concerns.

"Father, the hour has come," He begins. Into that hour is condensed the horrors that await Him. Previously, three times in the Gospel of John we read that His hour had not come (John 2:4; 7:30; and 8:20). The timing of His death is a reminder that the Crucifixion was neither an accident nor a tragedy that was tolerated by God. This hour was planned. The Son of man went "just as it is written of Him."

Marcus Rainsford said, "How long the Lord Jesus Christ *waited* upon His Father's will! For thirty years He lived in privacy; and now for nearly three and a half years, He has been engaged in public ministry. He had a baptism to be baptized with, and His soul was straitened till it was accomplished. Yet, He still awaits for His Father's appointed time to present Himself as a sacrifice for the sins of His people. What a picture of patience waiting upon God!"[1]

By what yardstick was His life measured? What could

He say now that His earthly existence was drawing to a close? What had motivated Him to be obedient to the Father's will?

■ A Right Motive

Christ makes only one request for Himself: "Glorify Thy Son" (17:1). He repeats the same request in verse 5, "And now glorify Thou Me together with Thyself, Father, with the glory which I had with Thee before the world was."

"Glorify Your Son." That word *glorify* means "to honor" or "to give due respect." But in this context, it's use is filled with irony. The glorification of Christ would take place through His shameful crucifixion. Far from praying for some selfish exaltation, He was actually asking that He might be faithful in the face of suffering and death. Earlier, Christ had explained to some Greeks who had come to see Him, "The hour has come for the Son of Man to be glorified. Truly, truly, I say to you, unless a grain of wheat falls into the earth and dies, it remains by itself alone; but if it dies, it bears much fruit" (12:23-24).

Though the cross was a symbol of violence and evil, to Christ it meant glory. It was the means God would use to reconcile a sinful world unto Himself. But it was through the humiliation of the Son that glory would be seen. As Carson said, "The manifestation of the glory of God . . . reaches its apex not in a blinding flash of resplendent light, but in the agony and triumph of the cross and empty tomb. To be sure, the Son would eventually be honored with the glory which He had before He appeared in Bethlehem. But the means to that glory was, humanly speaking, unattractive and painful."[2]

But why would Christ pray that He might be glorified? Was it for some selfish motive? Was it out of fear that He might be overlooked when He returned to the celestial heavens? No, He was primarily concerned about the Father's honor: "Glorify Thy Son, that Thy Son may glorify Thee." Christ is asking that the Father accept the work of the Son so that the Father's will in saving men and women would be accomplished. If Christ did not complete His mission or if the Father did not accept the sacrifice of the Son, Christ's assignment on earth would have ended in failure.

Let's not overlook the single-mindedness with which Christ served the Father. He had stayed clear of distractions; He had not been blown off course the by pressures of a controversial ministry. He served the Father with passionate focus. He was constantly in communion with the Father, making sure the divine will was being carried out. To Christ, nothing else mattered. And because of that single-mindedness, He could now say with confidence, "I have finished the work which Thou gavest Me to do."

But more precisely, how did Christ see His impending death as glorifying the Father? First, by His own obedience. Because Christ is God, we tend to think that He never faced the conflict of priorities like we do; we surmise that obedience to the Father was not difficult. But the New Testament paints a different picture. Paul, in motivating believers to please one another rather than themselves, said, "For even Christ did not please Himself" (Rom. 15:3). His was not the cheap obedience of a man unaffected by human emotions and exempt from moral conflict. Rather, Christ's choices were made in the face of emotional upheavals and the sting of rejection that came from His peers and His enemies. He was a man of sorrows and acquainted with grief. Yet, for all that, He obeyed. As He Himself said, "The Father hath not left Me alone, for I do always those things that please Him" (John 8:29, KJV).

Second, the choice to accept the cross glorified the

Father because it was so contrary to human values. That such a depressing scene as a crucifixion could be a means of glory boggles the mind. Christ had the faith to believe that an act should not be judged by the human eye; eternity cannot be seen this side of death. Eventually, He would be victorious, but He would have to hang unceremoniously between two thieves. To the casual observer, the man in the middle was no better off than the other two. Christ's willingness to be seen as a helpless failure was proof that He believed in the ultimate triumph of the Father's purposes.

All of us have seen believers die in depressing circumstances, sometimes after years of suffering in a deteriorating body. The family hovers close by, waiting for the end. Yet, perhaps, also denying that the end will ever come. The sanitary hospital rooms do not conceal the anguish in the face of those who suffer. It's difficult to seek glory amid the gasping of breath and the wrenching of pain. Yet, here, as in the death of Christ, there is the promise of glory. If we could but see the other side, we could accept our own death much more easily. We could have an Easter faith in a Good Friday world.

Paul, who saw more clearly than we the difference between time and eternity, said, "Therefore we do not lose heart, but though our outer man is decaying, yet our inner man is being renewed day by day. For momentary, light affliction is producing for us an eternal weight of glory far beyond all comparison, while we look not at the things which are seen, but at the things which are not seen; for the things which are seen are temporal, but the things which are not seen are eternal" (2 Cor. 4:16-18).

The humiliation of the moment can be more easily endured when seen in comparison with the glory of eternity. It's that ability to see glory in the ordinary depressing events of life that is called faith—and all men who please God must have it.

What does this say to us? Christ's one request for Himself was linked with His overriding desire to see the Father honored. His was a life lived with the priorities that we should adopt. Christ's motive was free from personal advantage. "But I do not seek My glory; there is One who seeks and judges" (John 8:50).

So His prayer to be glorified was not an end in itself but a means to a higher end, namely the glory of God the Father. Perhaps in·our motives more than anywhere else we are easily deceived. We are prone to pray for a large ministry so that the kingdom of heaven might be extended on earth. But behind that request may lie the baser motive; namely, the desire to be thought of as successful. Sometimes the most pious prayer requests disguise selfish motives. Even the committed may overlook such deceptions unless God is permitted to search the human heart.

If this week you have prayed, "Lord, bless me," you should have quickly added, "so that I may be able to bless You." Anything less is double-mindedness, a sin.

Why don't you ask God right now to show you your motives? I can warn you on the basis of personal experience that this can't be done in five minutes, or ten, or even twenty. It's only as we wait before the Lord that He will show us whether our prayers are for our own glory or His.

Christ made but one request for Himself, and His motivation was that, in the end, the Father would be glorified. Such a single-minded desire gladdens the heart of the Heavenly Father.

■ The Right Mission

Christ's single-mindedness made His many decisions easier. Since His overriding concern was the Father's will, He concentrated on doing those things that would fulfill the divine plan. D.L. Moody once said, "This one thing I do . . . and not these forty things I dabble in." Can you be that specific about why you are alive on this planet? I pray that such clarity of purpose would be true of you and me.

Here's the way Christ saw His job description: "Even as Thou gavest Him authority over all mankind, that to all whom Thou hast given Him, He may give eternal life." The expression "Those whom Thou hast given Him" is used six times in this prayer to refer to the elect, those whom God the Father chose to save. They were given to Christ by God the Father; these are the sheep for whom Christ would lay down His life.

In the Gospel of John, there is a great emphasis on God's sovereignty in election. Christ taught that He and the Father determined who would be saved. "For just as the Father raises the dead and gives them life, even so the Son also gives life to whom He wishes" (John 5:21).

However much we may be troubled by this mystery, we should not attempt to diminish the full force of Christ's words. He was sent on a rescue mission by God the Father to redeem those whom the Father had chosen. And then He could report that His work would soon be accomplished. By the end of the next day, His death would be over. Eternal life would have been purchased for the elect.

As for the eternal life which Christ gave to His people, we should notice first that it means much more than eternal existence. Even the wicked shall live forever. The phrase "eternal life" refers to the *quality* of existence. It's a life that has meaning and significance. It is not just life *from* God but the life *of* God.

As Christ made clear, a Christian is more than a sinner minus his sins; it's not just that our sins are forgiven but that we are given a necessary gift. "I give unto them eternal life." We need not be caught up by the passing fads of the world. For as David said, "Thou wilt make known to me the path of life; in Thy presence is fullness of joy; in Thy right hand there are pleasures forever-more" (Ps. 16:11).

The resurrection body of Christ gives us a glimpse of the kind of existence that awaits us after death. It's a life of glory, of power. It's a life of perpetual fulfillment and endless service to God.

Second, this life is connected with a personal knowledge of God. Throughout the Bible, a knowledge of God is considered the highest good that anyone could pursue. "He has told you, O man, what is good; and what does the Lord require of you but to do justice, to love kindness, and to walk humbly with your God?" (Micah 6:8) To walk with God—that is eternal life!

We should note in passing that this eternal life is a gift. It is, of course, the greatest gift that anyone could receive. It was purchased at high cost, but freely given to those who believe. Although we've all received gifts that we don't need at Christmastime, this is a necessary gift. Without it, no meaningful contact with God is possible.

Christ's mission, then, was to provide eternal life for those who believe. And this defines what one of our own priorities should be. Doing the will of God always involves bringing men and women to a saving knowledge of Christ. This, of course, can only be done because Christ finished the work the Father gave Him. Now He invites us to be partners in ministry, sharing the Good News of His fin-ished work.

■ The Right Milestone

Most of us live with regrets. We wish we could relive parts of our lives. Christ didn't have to look back wondering about such contingencies. He could say, "I have glorified Thee on the earth, having accomplished the work which Thou hast given Me to do" (v. 4). The next day, His humiliation on earth would reach its apex. He would say on the cross, "It is finished." The payment for sin will have been fully made.

Every event in Christ's life and death was planned. His experiences were a part of the eternal decree. It's almost as if God composed a musical drama that was played out day after day. When He came to the grave of Lazarus, He said, "Father, I thank Thee that Thou heardest Me. And I knew that Thou hearest Me always; but because of the people standing around I said it, that they may believe that Thou didst send Me" (John 11:41-42). Christ was saying, in effect, "Father, remember when You and I planned this hour long before I came to Bethlehem? ... Now, Lord, I know You are going to do what We agreed upon."

The cross itself was bittersweet. Bitter because of the pain and separation from God the Father; sweet because the Son's obedience pleased the Father. The author of Hebrews writes that Christ "who for the joy set before Him endured the cross, despising the shame, and has set down at the right hand of the throne of God" (Heb. 12:2). Beyond the humiliation there was exaltation.

Somewhere I read that when God pointed to the cross, He said, "This is what men think of My Son." But when He pointed to the Resurrection, He said, "This is what I think of My Son." So Christ the Son was fully vindicated.

How shall we measure the value of a life? Certainly not by its length, for Christ died when He was but thirty-three years old. Nor do we measure a life by whether someone dies easily. "He just slept away," I've heard people say about someone who died in his sleep. That's a pleasant way to go, but it doesn't guarantee that the life lived was a good one. Christ's death was violent. He did not have the luxury of "sleeping away." He died while His enemies walked past Him and jeered, while the blood flowed from His hands and side.

Nor should we measure a life on the basis of how well it was accepted by others. Official religion hated Christ. It was the religious leaders who put Him on the cross. If we think of the crucifixion and the scattering of the disciples, it most assuredly would appear that Christ's life was a failure.

How then shall we measure a life? It's whether our will agrees with God's will—whether we live our life for God's glory alone or for our own gratification. Surrendering to Christ means that we give up what is dear to us. Christ in His human nature also struggled against the blueprint that God had laid out for Him. "Now My soul has become troubled; and what shall I say, 'Father, save Me from this hour'? But for this purpose I came to this hour. Father, glorify Thy name" (John 12:27). To be surrendered to God's will is not easy; it involves a battle, conflict, agony.

If you are not aware that you are in a battle, then I seriously question the depth of your spiritual life. Satan and the flesh constantly pound away, trying to gain an advantage in our lives. Every inch is contested.

Christ died fulfilled because He had served the Father with the right motive; He had fulfilled the right mission; and He had reached the right milestone. But it wasn't easy for Him and it's not easy for us.

How does God help us separate the chaff from the wheat? Usually by a winnowing process, a sifting such as Peter experienced in Gethsemane. Unlike Christ, who was completely wheat, and Judas, who was completely chaff, Peter was a mixture of both. Let's not fight against the trials that help us separate the temporal from the eternal and the earthly from the heavenly. When the chips are down, God's glory should be all that matters, and nothing else.

After Peter Marshall's death, his wife Catherine said that at that moment she realized as never before that the value of a life consisted not in *duration* but in *donation*. It's not how *long* you live but *how* you live that matters.

Though Christ might not be considered successful by human standards, He pleased the Father, and that's all that mattered. And because of that submission, His task was finished. He had packed His bags and was ready to leave.

> Only one life, 'twill soon be passed,
> Only what's done for Christ will last.

If we want a whole heart in a broken world, we will have to have single-minded determination. Then we will be able to say with Christ, "I have finished what You gave Me to do."

NOTES

1. Rainsford, Marcus, *Our Lord Prays for His Own* (Chicago: Moody Press, 1950), pp. 39-40.
2. Carson, *The Farewell Discourse*, p. 177.

CHAPTER 11

KEEPING A SEPARATED HEART

JOHN 17:6-19

How long can you live with someone who is deceitful? That's the question a woman asked me last week. Her husband had never been completely honest and open to her in fifteen years of marriage. Many times she was confident that he was lying to her, but she could never quite prove it. Now she had discovered that he was not in the office after hours, but was seen with his secretary. Once again he denied it, trying to put her on a guilt trip with the "so-you-don't-trust-me" routine. Repeatedly he shunned her accusations.

Of all the sins most devastating to a marriage, adultery tops the list. The innocent partner feels rejected, grieved, and cheated. Sometimes it takes months, if not years, to restore the bond of security and trust that binds a marriage together. Adultery is so serious simply because marriage is so sacred. And when an adulterer lies, he only makes reconciliation more difficult.

Yet, there is another form of adultery that receives little attention—indeed it is considered quite respectable. James wrote, "You adultresses, do you not know that friendship with the world is hostility toward God? Therefore, whoever wishes to be a friend of the world makes himself an enemy of God" (James 4:4). In the Old Testament, God judged the nation Israel to be guilty of adultery because the people flirted with pagan gods.

To put it starkly: To be married to Christ (we are His bride) and to find our enjoyment in the world is to play the harlot. To be a Christian and to satisfy our lives with financial success, lust, or personal ambition is to betray the One whom we profess to love. Christ can never be misled with clever deception. He *knows* our hearts.

What does a wife who is in love with her husband and has no yen for another man do? She is not like the wife in a cartoon "Herman" who tells Herman, "What a coincidence! You forgot my birthday and I forgot how to cook!" No, the wife who loves her husband tries to please him, despite his shortcomings. She'll even buy the coffee he likes or make his favorite casserole. She works with her husband's interests in mind.

Similarly, when we are in love with Christ, we spend our energy "pleasing Him who has called us to be a soldier" (2 Timothy 2:3-4). What others say won't matter much—we'll just keep pleasing Him.

But Christians who love the world (or more accurately, *themselves*) will be concerned about what their friends are thinking. They'll go through life self-consciously asking: Did I make a good impression? Am I thought of as successful? Have I kept my reputation intact? They'll compare themselves with others and conclude that they are top-rate Christians.

To such believers, pleasing God is an impractical suggestion. They'd simply prefer to pay their dues—go to church, give occasional gifts to charity, and, above all, act respectably. Pleasing God is not their prime motivation. They have neither the time nor the inclination to seek first the kingdom of God and His righteousness.

Consider this: a wife in love with her husband will spend as much time as possible with him. She'll juggle her schedule and rearrange her priorities to be with her spouse. Lovers have an uncanny way of finding time to be together. As the saying reminds us, "Where there's a will, there's a way."

The analogy is obvious. Do we profess to love Christ? If so, was He on our mind yesterday? Do we readjust our schedules to make sure He has prime time on our priority lists? Remember, it's the Marys and not the Marthas who truly serve.

If we love the world, we will cram our lives full of everything but Christ. We'll choose good activities (remember, we want to be respectable Christians) and in the process push the Lord to the fringes of our lives. We don't have to commit great evils—indeed, we can pride ourselves on high standards. Yet, if the choice is between reading the Bible or watching TV; if we must choose between sharing our faith or remaining silent; if we face the decision of reading the daily newspaper or praying—we can predict what the outcome will be. When we lapse into carnality, God will be consulted only for emergencies.

Spiritual adultery is being married to Christ but finding thrills somewhere apart from Him. This explains why Christ prayed particularly that believers would be kept from the world. In John 17:6-19, He prays *that the believers might have contact with the world without the contamination of the world.*

This form of separation means more than simply saying no to movies, dancing, drinking, and smoking. Certainly, it includes the renunciation of all worldly practices, but even more importantly, Christ wants our hearts to be separated unto Him. The most important part of us is the part that no one ever sees—except God. And that's the part that God wants us to keep from evil.

Christ prays for the disciples because they belong mutually to the Father and the Son—"and all things that are Mine are Thine, and Thine are Mine; and I have been glorified in them" (v. 10). That God's honor (in the sight of men) is linked to the success or failure of the disciples elevates them to a special status. So our Lord earnestly prays that His disciples would be kept from the pollution of the world.

He does not mention the disciples' failures. Nothing is said regarding the misunderstanding, bickering, and fear that they exhibited from time to time. Instead, Christ says, "I have been glorified in them" (v. 10). So now He commits them to the Father for safekeeping.

What does Christ mean when He says "keep them"? He's asking that they will be kept in unity, that they will be kept in the Father's love, and that they will be pure in their relationships to the world. He knows that having a pure heart in a dirty world will necessitate supernatural keeping power. The evil within us often joins forces with the evil that exists without, and together they seek to destroy us; so He prays, "Keep them."

■ Keep Them in Unity

"Keep them in Thy name, the name which Thou hast given Me, that they may be one even as We are" (v. 11). The unity Christ prays about is the spiritual unity that became a reality on the Day of Pentecost. Christ knew that dark forces would soon attempt to break up His band of men. They had to be protected from their own individual plans so that they could be fully obedient to Christ's mission. Since Pentecost, all believers have been indwelt and baptized by the Holy Spirit. "For by one Spirit are we all baptized into one body whether we be Jews or Greek, whether we be bond or free and have been all made to drink of one Spirit" (1 Cor. 12:13). Unfortunately, the baptism of the Spirit that unites us today is a cause of great division in the church. But the point is that there is a spiritual unity that transcends all other differences among Christians.

This unity is based on truth. We can't fulfill Christ's prayer by getting all denominations together in an attempt to present a united front to the world. Getting several cemeteries together does not produce a resurrection! Christ based the unity on the fact that these disciples had received His word; they knew who He was and responded to the truth.

We ask: Was this prayer fulfilled? We know that God granted Christ an answer to His prayers, but we might be tempted to suspect that this one was left unanswered. Look at all the denominations—Baptists, Methodists, Mennonite, and Independents, just to name a few. Certainly in this century, we can say that the church does not seem to be one!

But there is a fundamental unity among those who belong to Jesus Christ. Unfortunately, we tend to magnify our disagreements and often forget that true believers have much that unites them. We disagree about matters such as infant baptism, eternal security, or the structure of church government. These differences are important, but yet there is a unity among those who have been born again of the Holy Spirit. In some instances, some denominations have left the true faith; yet even among them there are at least some individuals who know Christ personally and with whom we can fellowship. At any rate, there is a unity among the people of God and it is our responsibility "to keep the unity of the Spirit in the bond of peace."

Without unity, we become an easy prey for the devil. If sheep wish to be protected from the wolves, they must stay with the flock. Christ never assumed that anyone could live the Christian life on his own. Every individual believer is a member of the body of Christ and must function within that body, interacting with other believers. Unless we are knit together in love, we cannot enter into the fullness of Christ. No person can live unto himself and die unto himself.

In Africa, a two-year-old child wandered off into the forest. The entire tribe spent the day searching for this youngster but could not find him. The next day, they decided to join hands and cover the entire area. They found the boy, but unfortunately, he was dead after having spent the night outside. The distraught mother cried, "Why didn't we hold hands before?"

Christ prayed that we would hold hands. We need one another within the body. A man who struggled with pornography for many years in desperation shared his need with a few Christian friends who began to uphold him consistently in prayer. Almost instantly, he was completely delivered from this sinful practice. Why? It's because there is *strength within the body*. That's why Christ prayed that we would be one and that our unity would enable us to confront the world.

■ Keep Them Securely

The keeping for which Christ prayed also involves the security of believers. "While I was with them, I was keeping them in Thy name which Thou hast given Me; and I guarded them, and not one of them perished, but the son of perdition, that the Scripture might be fulfilled" (v. 12).

This means more than physical safety. He wants the disciples to be kept by God forever. Salvation for those who believe is secure, because it is a free gift. And Paul writes that "the gifts and the calling of God are irrevocable" (Rom. 11:29). The Lord didn't make the down payment for salvation and then expect us to keep up with the installments. If I cannot be saved as a result of my good works, I cannot lose my salvation as a result of my bad works.

Salvation is of God. He desires to save those whom He has given to Christ as a gift. It's inconceivable that any one of them would be lost.

But what about Judas? Christ says that none of the ones that He guarded perished—"but the son of perdition, that the Scripture might be fulfilled" (v. 12). Let's not read this verse as if it says that Christ kept all that the Father gave Him but wasn't able to hang on to Judas! Judas was not kept because he was never given to the Son of God by the Father. Christ knew that Judas was an imposter. "Did I Myself not choose you, the Twelve, and yet one of you is a devil?" He asked (John 6:70). Earlier, we noted that Christ said that Judas was not among those who were clean (13:10).

Not a single one given by God the Father to God the Son will be lost. Judas is not an example of someone who lost his salvation; he's an example of a hypocrite who pretended to have salvation but didn't. God is well able to keep His people saved!

What would you think of a shepherd who left in the morning with 100 sheep but came back in the evening with 95? He would be the laughingstock of the town. A good shepherd brings the same number of sheep home in the evening as he had in the morning. Christ is truly the Good Shepherd.

■ Kept in Purity

Christ said, "Sanctify them in the truth; Thy word is truth" (v. 17). Sanctification is the personal holiness for which Christ prays. It's not merely negative—namely, that the disciples will be kept from sin. It is also positive—that they will be set apart by God for the responsibility of winning the world. That's why Christ can pray, "I sanctify Myself" (v. 19). Obviously, Christ was sinless. So He wasn't praying that He would be set apart from sin, but rather that He would be set apart to do the Father's work.

The disciples must be kept from Satan's subtle traps to live distinctly for God. Tertulian said that at the end of the second century, the pagans railed against the Christians. "How long must we put up with this third race?" they stormed. The church was so distinct from the world, that it made its mark.

The church is to be in the world like a ship is in the ocean. But when the ship begins to take on water, it begins to sink. Yet, if we as believers cannot stay afloat, how can we have the strength to rescue those who are drowning around us?

To continue the ship analogy: Christ prayed that there would be unity on the ship, not mutiny. He also prayed that the disciples would be secure—that their ship would arrive at the harbor, no matter how many storms it had along the way. And He also prayed that no water would get into the ship—purity is what He desired for His people. Christ, who prayed these words for His disciples, most probably prays similar prayers for us today as our High Priest. He is before the Father as our representative. When the church falls in love with the world, He is grieved. His ultimate purposes will be accomplished, but our divided affections touch Him deeply. To love the world is to not love God.

To have a whole heart is to have a separated heart. Compromise with the world brings division and fragmentation. To be separated unto God fosters emotional wholeness.

CHAPTER 12

PRESERVING A COMMITTED HEART

JOHN 17:20-26

In a published Easter message titled "Never Again to Die," Earnest Campbell tells of a grave marker in an old cemetery in Girard, Pennsylvania. The inscription reads:

> In memory of
> Ellen Shannon
> aged 26 years
> who was fatally burned
> March 21, 1870
> by the explosion of a lamp
> filled with R.E. Danforth's
> non-explosive
> burning fluid

Campbell goes on to say that he is tired of nonexplosive fluids exploding; of fail-proof banks that fail; of surefire programs that fall flat. He is tired of preventatives that don't prevent, of solutions that do not solve, of remedies that do not cure, of panaceas that don't pan out.[1]

Yes, we are all tired of promises that are not kept, and of cures that disappoint. Christ has given us a message that is guaranteed to work. He backs His promises by His own character and the power of deity. He is well qualified to "save forever those who draw near to God through Him, since He always lives to make intercession for them" (Heb. 7:25).

Christ is not only able to reconcile us to God, but to reconcile us to other people and to ourselves. In an age of hurt, there is emotional and spiritual healing. Christ has had much experience in healing the brokenhearted and setting at liberty those who are bruised. Someone has said, "He can make you whole if you give Him all the pieces."

In John 17, Christ prayed for His disciples. He knew that they would not be able to meet the deep needs of others until they themselves had their own hurts healed. A life-changing message must be built on the foundation of an authentic life. To put it differently: it is difficult to rescue someone from drowning if you yourself are going under!

Of course, not one of us has it completely "all together." As one wag put it, "When I finally got it all together, I found I couldn't lift it!" We are all in different stages of spiritual growth, but none of us is able to help others beyond our own experience.

Yet with all our failures, Christ has given us the greatest responsibility in the world. The President of the United States has a little black box that goes with him; it's a box that contains the combination that could begin a nuclear war. A big responsibility indeed, but no greater than that which rests with us. Although Christ made it clear that God's elect would be saved, it is equally clear that we have the responsibility of preaching the Gospel to everyone. On the divine side, the salvation of men and women is in

God's hands; but humanly speaking, the fate of men and women is in our hands. However much we may struggle with this paradox, the fact remains that we have the responsibility of sharing the Gospel that can change a person's destiny forever. We don't have a box, but we do have a book that can unlock the human heart.

As we've already learned, *we are to take Christ's place in the world.* "As Thou didst send Me into the world, I also have sent them into the world" (v. 18). Now that He was leaving, the disciples would represent Him to the human race. Just as a president may delegate certain responsibilities to his vice president, so Christ asked us to be His representatives. We take over where He left off.

In John 17, as mentioned earlier, Christ prays for Himself in verses 1 through 5; in verses 6 through 19, He prays for His disciples; and in verses 20 through 26 He prays for all of us. Every believer is remembered by Him. Six times He prays that "we may be one." This is not a uniformity that is imposed from the outside; it is the unity of the supernatural life that has been implanted within us. Although in one sense, it is a completed unity (by the baptism of the Holy Spirit), it is also a unity that is progressive. Christ prayed that "they may be perfected in unity" (v. 23). It's a unity that is already a fact, but one that must also continually progress.

If we are to help men and women in this broken world, we must be clear about our resources and privileges. Speaking to a woman who had been sexually abused by her stepfather, I asked what one truth helped her the most in putting the past behind her. Next to God granting her the ability to forgive, she said it was the fact that she was unconditionally loved by God.

To be as precious to God the Father as Jesus Christ, is indeed a most comforting truth.

Ponder this: you share the same honor, future, and love from God the Father as does Christ Himself! Even if you can't entertain such a thought, accept it by faith. For this is precisely what Christ's prayer teaches.

■ We Share the Same Honor

Christ, now praying for us, says, "And the glory which Thou hast given Me I have given them that they may be one, just as We are one" (v. 22).

The glory that God the Father gave to God the Son we ourselves now receive. What could this possibly mean? There are two kinds of glory. We have the glory of the cross that Jesus experienced while doing the Father's will on earth. As Donald Carson says, "The glory the Father gave the Son was the glory of the humility of the Incarnation, culminating both in the glorification of the Son at the Crucifixion and in the glory of His resurrected and exalted state."[2] The glory, then, is that we follow the way of the cross. William Barclay has pointed out that we should never think of the Cross as our penalty but rather as our glory. The harder the task we give a student or a craftsman, the more we honor him. So although it is hard to live the Christian life, we must regard it as our glory and honor.

We've all heard someone say, "Everyone has a cross to bear." For some it might be a rebellious child, for another unemployment, or yet for another arthritis or heart disease. But these kinds of trials are shared by all of us. Someone has observed that whenever a non-Christian gets cancer, God also allows a Christian to get cancer so that the world can tell the difference! But Christ was referring to the stigma associated with our witness in the world. The ridicule we receive from our identification with Him is "our cross."

But this cross is also our glory. When the apostles were beaten, lacerated, and threatened, they returned to their friends "rejoicing that they had been considered worthy to suffer shame for His name" (Acts 5:41). *That* is glory.

Here again we see a sharp distinction between the values of the world and the values of Christ. The world regards all difficulty as evil and undesirable. The cross is to be avoided at all costs. But a Christian looks at the trials of life differently; he sees them as entering into the sufferings of Christ.

There is, of course, a second kind of glory that is intrinsic to the Godhead. Although we do not have that kind of glory which is reserved for Christ, we do share the glory of His suffering. And that is a privilege we receive when we stand up for Christ in the middle of a wicked, unbelieving world. And just as the Father was pleased with Christ's obedience, so He is pleased with ours too—as we continue to walk in the footsteps of the Saviour.

Treat other believers with respect and love. For Christ shares His honor with them.

We all like to be seen with people whom we admire. Years ago, I attended a Cubs baseball game in Chicago. I noticed that Don Kessinger, the all-star shortstop, was constantly surrounded by fans the moment he was off the field. They wanted his picture and autograph, hoping that some of the glory would rub off.

Christ would have been glad to have the disciples photographed with Him! Though there is an unbridgable gap between Christ and His followers, He is not ashamed to call us "brothers," His special friends. To cement the relationship between Himself and us, Christ prayed that the glory He received would be given to us. Every time we represent Him in the world, we participate in that glory.

■ We Share the Same Future

Now Christ continues, "Father, I desire that they also, whom Thou hast given Me, be with Me where I am, in order that they may behold My glory, which Thou has given Me; for Thou didst love Me before the foundation of the world" (v. 24). Here Christ uses the second definition of the word *glory*. He speaks of the glory that He had with the Father before the world was. Through the Incarnation, this aspect of Christ's glory was shielded from us. But in that day, the limitations will be set aside—the curtain will be pulled back. When we get to heaven, we will see Him as He is. The transfiguration is a dress rehearsal, a preview of eternity. There Christ's body was changed into a glorious body to help the disciples understand His deity and commitment to the coming kingdom. Earlier in this book, we noted that He promised to take the disciples back with Him to glory. However much we might love Christ now; however much we may behold His glory on the pages of the New Testament, all this is but dimness in comparison to the revealed glory we shall behold in the future. Theologians refer to this ultimate bliss as the *Visio Dei:* the vision of God. As Carson says, "Without it, heaven would be an empty triumph."

> Face to face with Christ my Saviour
> Face to face, what will it be
> When with rapture I behold Him
> Jesus Christ who died for me?
>
> Only faintly now I see Him,
> With the darkening veil between;
> But a blessed day is coming,
> When His glory shall be seen.

Using the word *glory* in these two senses, Christ can say

He has given us His glory, but He can also pray that we might see His glory in the future. It's the paradox of our glory on earth in sharing His sufferings and the glory of who He is as a member of the Trinity. Some honors do rightfully belong only to Christ, others He gives to us.

Almost every church today has its problems. The seven letters to the churches found in Revelation are a microcosm of the church today. There is in each something to be praised and something to be rectified. Every church is a mixture of wheat and chaff. What would a church do that was completely free of the frailty of the flesh and the imperfections of doctrine? What would a church be like that was indeed perfect, that was composed only of believers, all of whom desired only the glory and praise of God? No criticisms, no power plays, no doctrinal arguments. Such a church cannot be found on earth. You'll recall the old adage: "If you ever find a perfect church and join it, it will be perfect no longer."

But in the Book of Revelation there is a picture of such a church and its primary activity is worshiping in the presence of God.

And when the living creatures give glory and honor and thanks to Him who sits on the throne, to Him who lives forever and ever, the twenty-four elders will fall down before Him who sits on the throne, and will worship Him who lives forever and ever, and will cast their crowns before the throne, saying, "Worthy art Thou, O Lord and our God, to receive glory and honor and power; for Thou didst create all things, and because of Thy will they existed and were created" (Rev. 4:9-11).

It is for this future prospect that Christ prays. There we

shall be before Him with complete moral and spiritual agreement, exempt from the limitations of the flesh. At last the desire of Christ and the motives of His people will converge: together we shall exist in fellowship and harmony forever. Beholding Christ's glory and worshiping Him will be the fulfillment of our own longings and dreams.

As a believer, be careful who you pick a fight with—perhaps you will be standing next to that person in the divine choir! Surely the Lord is grieved when personalities and lesser issues fragment the impact of His body on earth. The unity for which Christ prays is the bridge which links His power with the world.

Not long ago, I spoke with a couple filled with despair. Although they are middle-aged, both are experiencing physical handicaps; they feel rejected by their friends and their church. As I listened to their many complaints, I couldn't help but think of the future glory that awaits those who are faithful even in the midst of the harsh realities of life. Yes, Christians are imperfect. Yes, we do all suffer from the trials of life. Yet, the glory awaits us. That prospect helps us when our worlds collapse.

■ We Share the Same Love

As parents, it is difficult for us to love each of our children equally. Though we tell ourselves that we do not have a favorite child, it's difficult to love each of our children alike. Christ is the unique Son of God. Because the Father loved Him so supremely, He gave Him the Holy Spirit without measure. There was no limit to the Father's resources given to the Son, because the Son pleased the Father, and the Father loved Him with intensity and unfailing devotion. Indeed, the relationship between them is one characterized by love. As God the Father said, "This is My beloved Son in whom I am well pleased."

Yet, we too are sons of God in a secondary sense. Here again we must bear in mind the distinction between Christ and His followers, but we must also see the similarities. Christ reminds the Father, "Thou . . . didst love them, even as Thou didst love Me" (v. 23b).

Notice that as the Father loved the Son, so He loves us. The extent of that love can, to some degree, be grasped mentally, but not emotionally. Even as I write these words, it is difficult for me to accept Christ's statement that I am loved as much as He is. I understand the words, but I find it hard to accept the truth.

Those who see themselves as failures, those who lack significance in this world; indeed all of us would experience emotional and spiritual strength if we remember that the Father's special favor rests upon us.

And how *long* has the Father loved us? Christ said that the Father loved Him "before the foundation of the world." That's true also of His love for us. The Father, who loved the Son from eternity past, also loves those whom He has chosen; that is, He loves those whom He has given to Christ as a gift from all eternity. He has set His love on us long before we knew Him. When we were yet without strength, in due time Christ died for the ungodly. Paul says in Ephesians, "Just as He chose us in Him before the foundation of the world, that we should be holy and blameless before Him" (1:4).

Sin always fragments. It divides families and nations. A child is set against his parents, a wife against her husband. But love unites; it brings us together. And that's the love that brings us into favor with God and union forever in His presence. "I have made Thy name known to them, and will make it known; that the love wherewith Thou didst love Me may be in them, and I in them" (v. 26).

God has given us all the resources we need to take

Christ's place in the world. We have been sent into the world just as He was sent. As God the Father supplied all that Christ needed to accomplish His mission, so God supplies all that we need. If I send one of my daughters to buy groceries, I am responsible to give her the money that she needs. Along with my command to purchase potatoes, meat, and corn, comes the money to pay for these items. When Christ told His disciples that He was sending them into the world, He prayed that they might have such a close relationship with Him that all of His resources might be theirs.

Just think of how God has honored us. He has shared Christ's glory, future, and love with us. The resources are there if we have the will to obey.

If we allow the sins of the world to clog the flow of spiritual life, it's like putting water in a kerosene stove. The flame will flutter and eventually go out. It produces neither light nor heat. When we allow water in our spiritual fuel tank, we lose our impetus. Christ has given us the fuel; our responsibility is to make sure we do not grieve the Spirit and thereby dissipate His power.

Once more we remind ourselves that we are Christ's representatives in the world. A little girl once asked her father why firemen had to stay in the firehouse all day polishing their engines. He explained that this was done to pass the time while waiting for fire calls. That's like many Christians who stay close to the familiar surroundings of the church community, applying another coat of sanctification or getting a theological tune-up, all the while waiting for some sinner to request a Gospel presentation. Yet the world is ablaze around us, whether it calls for our help or not. They will not care that our paint job is dull or that our engine sputters as long as we bring them to Christ. Staying in the firehouse awaiting a call is all right for firemen, but we Christians need to go out and do the work.

Someone has written:

We are the only Bible
The careless world will read
We are the sinner's gospel.
We are the scoffer's creed.
We are the Lord's last message
Given in deed and word.
What if the type is crooked?
What if the print is blurred?

We don't choose whether we want to represent Christ in the world. For good or for ill, we *do* represent Him. "As the Father hath sent Me, so send I you."

When Abraham Lincoln dedicated the cemetery at Gettysburg, where so many soldiers lost their lives, he said:

We cannot dedicate, we cannot consecrate, we cannot hallow this ground. The brave men who struggled here have consecrated it far beyond our power to add or detract. It is for us, the living, rather, to be dedicated to the great task remaining before us, that from these honored dead we might take increased devotion to that cause for which they gave the last full measure of devotion, and that we here highly resolve that these dead shall not have died in vain.

Neither can we add nor detract from what Christ has done. Yet we must be dedicated to the great task remaining before us. The love of Christ should be our motivation to represent Him effectively and accurately to the world.

Christ offers the world a reason to live and a cause for which to die. He's the Healer of hearts, the Saviour of souls.

It's up to us to spread the Word.

NOTES

1. Campbell, Earnest, "Never to Die Again," published in *The Miracle of Easter,* Floyd Thatcher, (ed.), (Waco, Texas: Word Books, 1980), p. 41.
2. Carson, *The Farewell Discourse,* p. 197.